CHANCES AND CHOICES

CHANCES
AND
CHOICES

Making Integration Work

Deborah Fullwood

·P·A·U·L·H·
BROOKES
PUBLISHING Cº

Baltimore · London · Toronto · Sydney

Paul H. Brookes Publishing Co.
PO Box 10624
Baltimore, Maryland 21285-0624

Copyright © 1990 by MacLennan & Petty Pty Limited

Printed and bound in Australia

Illustrations by Leah Winterton

Library of Congress Cataloging-in-Publication Data
Fullwood, Deborah.
    Chances and choices: making integration work/Deborah Fullwood.
        p.   cm.
    Includes bibliographical references.
    ISBN 1-55766-055-7
    1. Rehabilitation.   2. Handicapped children–Education.
I. Title.
HV1568.F85   1990
371.9-dc20   90-1331
                                                                          CIP

CONTENTS

PREFACE

Chances and Choices aims to provide a useful, rational approach towards overcoming the many practical and social dilemmas which can be experienced in the integration of a person with a disability into ordinary community activities. In this book 'integration' is defined as 'a process which offers a person who has a disability the same chances and choices as other people to participate in life's activities and to become a full member of life's communities'. A community is defined as 'a group of people who come together for a common purpose and who are needed to maintain that purpose.... A community includes all its participants, no matter their role: bosses, staff, volunteers, people participating in the community's activities and their families'. A disability is defined as 'a restriction or lack of ability in performing an activity in the usual way'. Some people have a minimal disability; some people have severe and multiple disabilities that handicap them in many ways.

Through both my professional and personal involvement with integration, I have spoken with many people and I am amazed at their wealth of experience. Integration is no longer just a paper dream with only academic arguments or untried strategies to support it; integration is a reality that is here to stay. It is a social process whose underlying principle of justice and equal chances and choices for everyone remains firm, despite changes over time, through differing circumstances and across different communities.

This is a positive book, a practical book of optimism and action. It isn't a do-it-yourself manual, a fix-it for problems, a debate between integration and segregation, a personal account or a deep and meaningful essay on the pros and cons of integration. If anything, it is a self-help book.

In *Chances and Choices* I have tried to avoid value judgements, and have tried instead to raise awareness and to provide information and options. I have focused on explaining both the issues that surround integration and their impact on attitudes, rather than on exploring them individually in depth. I have also tried to avoid a 'right or wrong' approach in discussing attitudes or strategies. Instead I have outlined people's different perspectives and the resultant range of attitudes, but also emphasised that community members with a range of attitudes have all been part of communities that have made integration work.

Similarly I have emphasised the range of organisational models that have made integration work. Policies and strategies that suit one community may not entirely suit another, but basic factors are common to successful integration, no matter how uniquely each community interprets and implements them. Any practical or interactional strategies suggested keep as their focus the individuality of each situation. The perspective of people who have a disability is not directly addressed but is maintained through an emphasis on the individuality of the chances they take and the choices they make.

Chances and Choices presumes that readers have some interest in integration—this may or may not be involvement with, or commitment to, integration. The book has particular relevance to parents and caregivers of people who have a disability and to professionals working with them towards integration—perhaps these are the people most strongly motivated to make integration work. However it is also very relevant for staff at regular communities, for people who have a disability and, indeed, for all people—we are all community members of one sort or another. Regardless of the type of community under consideration, or the severity and complexity of a person's disabilities, *Chances and Choices* has something to offer. Hopefully a reader's interest extends to not only understanding integration, what it offers and how it happens, but also to a desire to play a personal part in making integration work.

A glossary has been provided to clarify colloquiallisms and to identify and clarify terms as they are used in this book, encouraging further reading. Quotes which are not referenced result from interviews for either this book or for my previous book *Facing the Crowd*, from discussions with colleagues and friends, through my personal and professional experiences in the area of integration and from overheard comments. The perspective of the quoted speaker is identified in situations where this is necessary—'a parent' means the parent of a person with a disability. Names in the quotes have been altered to provide some continuity for the reader:

- The person with the disability is called 'John' or 'Jane'.
- The parental partners of the person with the disability are called 'Pam' or 'Paul'.
- Various siblings are called 'Simon', 'Susan' or 'Sally'.
- 'Simon' has a girlfriend called 'Gail'.
- 'Mr and Mrs Leader', and 'Mr and Mrs Staff' are boss and staff member, respectively, of the community.

The book is divided into parts ('ready', 'set', 'go' and 'keep going') which together support the philosophy that integration is not static, but a process that can be developed through the efforts of individuals. It is a process that can be prepared for, managed and kept going.

Integration means not just being together, but doing activities together. Integration is not just polite attendance at a community or participation in its activities; it also implies interaction and interdependence between community members. Integration means being part of a community, belonging to the community. It is not just having a job, but getting a real wage for real work; it is not just attending the local school with peers, but learning with them; it is not just joining the local scout group, but going on camp and doing duty on carwash day with them; it is not just going to the pub with friends, but shouting a round of drinks.

Integration—chances and choices for everyone.

Deborah Fullwood

ACKNOWLEDGEMENTS

My sincere appreciation extends Australia-wide to all those people who have, sometimes unwittingly, shared with me their experiences, ideas, hopes and concerns about integration. Their experiences add the richness and variety to this book.

I am also appreciative of the time, effort and interest shown by the people who read the draft and added comments from their various perspectives.

I must gratefully acknowledge the generosity of the Royal Victorian Institute for the Blind, Melbourne, Australia, who agreed to my use in this book of some material and ideas from *Facing the Crowd* which I had previously co-authored for them.

I am indebted, as in most things, to Andrew.

FOREWORD

The basic premise of this book is that there is a growing recognition of and respect for 'social justice and equality'. As defined by Ms. Fullwood, this movement accepts that all persons should be equally valued, provided equal opportunities, viewed as unique individuals, and be exposed to and learn from and about people with diverse characteristics. These principles are becoming guiding forces for integration in schools and society. Such a view of integration goes beyond physical proximity to the need to develop and maintain inclusive schools and communities in which every person is welcomed, valued, and expected to support as well as be supported by his or her fellow members.

This growing movement has far-reaching implications and can provide positive insights in how to accept and approach people in society who have been labelled as having a disability. Generally, people with disabilities have *not* had the principles of social justice or equality applied to them. That is, for far too long they have been 'devalued' citizens (Wolfensberger, 1983), considered 'better off' separated from their community peers.

However, through parent involvement, self-advocacy by persons labelled disabled, and the activity of other disability rights advocates, such views are beginning to change. The basic rights of people with disabilities to equal access and opportunities in the mainstream of educational and community life are being recognised and accepted. Attitudes, laws, and practices are beginning to change to reflect this forward movement.

While equality in terms of human rights has been the driving force behind many of the integration advances, increasing momentum is also being gained as a result of the positive impact that integration has brought about. The benefits to *all* persons when previously excluded people are included are being recognised. Persons labelled disabled are beginning to be recognised as unique, valued individuals with a wealth of gifts and talents to contribute to their educational and social communities. They are being recognised as sources of support rather than only recipients of support. Persons with disabilities who have previously been denied participation in the mainstream are an important and valuable part of the community and an untapped resource that society no longer can afford to exclude or neglect.

However, to achieve totally inclusive schools and communities in which everyone is welcome, valued, and supported, and to which everyone contributes, much still needs to be done. Advocacy, attitude change, and expanded availability of appropriate programs, supports, and services within schools and communities that allow everyone to participate and contribute in a meaningful way are still needed. In *Chances and Choices*, Ms. Fullwood provides generous insight into the process of moving forward to achieve both equity and excellence for all people, labelled 'disabled' or not, in educational and other community settings. She brings the perspective of both a parent of a child with disabilities and a service provider to students who have experienced exclusion from the educational and community mainstream. *Chances and Choices* is a book that has much to offer its readers in gaining an understanding of and directions for achieving equality among all members of society.

Parents always have been at the forefront of the integration movement. Now Ms. Fullwood has written a book that clearly outlines how many more parents, educators, and community members can become actively involved in assisting people who have a disability to become integrated into their communities. As noted above, she is a parent herself and this may be why this book goes straight to the central issues involved and provides practical approaches to overcome the barriers to social justice and equality for all. With this book in hand, families and those people who support them will be in a much better position in their struggle to achieve inclusive classrooms and communities where everyone is welcomed and valued.

Susan Stainback, Ed. D.
William Stainback, Ed. D.
Professors of Education
University of Northern Iowa
Cedar Falls

REFERENCE

Wolfensberger, W. (1983). Social role valorization: A proposed new term for the principle of normalization. *Mental Retardation, 21*, 234–239.

PART ONE: **READY?**

Part one provides the background to integration: an understanding of what integration is, why it should happen and how it can work. These chapters are vital for understanding ideas in later chapters; they provide a direction and purpose to the practical and personal efforts that may be needed to make integration work.

Part one also provides a number of perspectives, which promotes an understanding of other people's opinions and feelings about integration. An understanding of the perspective of other people in a similar role (a parent, a staff or community member) helps a person clarify his or her own perspective. Additionally, knowledge about the different perspectives of people in other roles generates a broader understanding of the issues that surround integration. Such understanding helps explain why integration is sometimes rough going; it identifies areas where views diverge and where acknowledgement of these diverse viewpoints must be made if integration is to work.

Importantly, acknowledgement of personal hopes and concerns, and recognition of those of other people, allows planning that addresses these feelings but still keeps as its focus the needs of the person with the disability.

Understanding integration helps people get ready to make it work.

Chapter One

WHAT IS INTEGRATION?

What is all the fuss about? What *is* integration? It is not something extra-ordinary or even very new and it should not be something about which people feel afraid. Integration is about people with a disability having the same chances and choices in life as other people. Although the concept of integration is simple, finding a simple definition and putting integration into practice can be more complicated. That is what all the fuss is about.

Through history, the word 'integration' has referred to the involvement of people from minority groups in situations where a basic right has been taken for granted by the majority. In the late 19th century 'integration' referred to the inclusion of poor students into the education system. In the 1960s it referred to the access of people of any race to common facilities—schools, restaurants and suburbs. In the 1980s integration is often used to refer to the integration of people who have a disability into ordinary life activities, and that is the purpose of this book.

Integration is difficult to define partly because it is a process rather than a fixed state; likewise integration is not a polarised situation where either it is undeniably happening or it is not happening at all. Another difficulty is that the process of integration is composed of many levels of relationships including both the physical (people being together and participating in community activities) and the social (people interacting and being inter-dependent).

In everyday conversations people frequently use the word 'integration': 'This is an integrated computer system', 'The new building materials integrate well in the old house'. In both these examples, 'integration' has meanings of 'being an important part of the whole' and 'blending in'. Integration has the same meanings when it is used in connection with people who have a disability. In this book 'integration' means a process which offers a person who has a disability the same chances and choices as other people to participate in life's activities and to become a full member of life's communities.

'Integration' is based on the word 'integrity' which can mean 'to be yourself among others, able and allowed to be yourself among others'. It does not mean 'making identical' or even 'making similar', and neither does it mean making people conform, pass a certain standard or be 'more normal'. It doesn't mean hiding differences. However, integration does

3

mean *allowing* people to be the same if they want to, through giving them the same chances and choices in their lives.

As well as the right to be the same, integration recognises people's right to be different. It recognises that people need a variety of experiences in order to make a genuine choice, particularly when their choice is different to the one most people would make. A variety of experiences allows a person to make a *real* choice based on experience. Otherwise a person may choose to be 'different' just because he has not been allowed to be 'the same', or because he has not had the opportunity to see other people's lives and to know how different are his own choices.

A teenager may choose second-hand Op-shop clothes to wear rather than modern, punk or conservative fashions. She may be from a minority group—black or poor or have a disability—and can be expressing her individuality from among the range of clothes that she knows teenagers wear. Another teenager, who has a disability, may also dress in second-hand clothes but she may do so because that is all she is offered (she is given no choice), or because she is only familiar with out-of-date clothes (perhaps all the other teenagers at her community house wear out-of-date clothes). She may not realise how unusual her choice is. Despite wearing the same clothes, the first teenager's choice reflects the notion of integration, but the second teenager's choice does not.

Integration allows people to be individual and it also allows communities to be individual. In this book a 'community' means a group of people who come together for a common purpose and who are needed to maintain that purpose. A school is a community and so is a neighbourhood, club, shopping centre, workplace or childcare centre. A community includes all its participants, no matter their role: bosses, staff, volunteers, people participating in the community's activities and their families. A school community would include all the teaching and administration staff, students, parents and volunteers.

Integration doesn't aim to change the purpose, rules or regulations of communities or to make them all alike; that would defeat its purpose by reducing the variety of environments in which a person could choose to participate. However, while acknowledging the differences between communities, integration aims to ensure that within each community all members have the same chances and choices.

Integration doesn't imply that no 'special services' should be available for use by people who have a disability. What it *does* imply is that a choice is available to them, a choice which includes a variety of special services and regular community services available in a variety of segregated and regular community locations. Because people are individuals and have individual abilities and difficulties, they will make different choices; they will differ in the amount of 'special' assistance they choose and need, and in where they want to receive any special services they do choose. Additionally, the same person may choose differing amounts of special assistance for different aspects of his life: such as living independently while working at a sheltered workshop, or living in a community residential unit but working in open employment, or attending a regular school but using recreation clubs for people with a disability.

People without a disability also use special services from time to time—they buy fast food instead of cooking a meal themselves or use a taxi rather than taking a train. They choose these 'special services' because they were the most suitable at the time, just like special services suit people with a disability sometimes.

Although integration can refer to any community activity it often refers to schooling: 'Has that deaf child been integrated?', 'Does Murrayville High School take disabled integrated students?'. 'Educational integration' has developed a high profile in Australia, and most state governments have developed policies (and sometimes legislation) to address the issues of education for students with a disability in regular schools.

In Australia as in many other countries, equal opportunity legislation exists to protect the rights of many minority groups (women, people with a disability, people from particular ethnic or religious groups) in many situations (work, housing, shopping, recreation or education). Communities outside education (like sporting clubs, churches and shopping centres) have rarely felt the need for additional legislation specifically about the right of people with a disability to join their communities. Perhaps this is because communities outside education have also rarely felt the need to establish separate facilities for people with a disability. If a person with a disability wants to shop or go to church, she usually goes where people without a disability also shop or go to church.

In comparison, if a person with a disability wants to get an education, she *may* be able to attend a school catering for children without a disability and she *certainly* can attend a school designed for children with a disability. A complete and separate education system has been established for people who have a disability. In the past, to get an education where children without a disability were educated was seen as odd, inappropriate and (shock! horror!) radical! Rules and regulations were developed to stop too much of it happening!

In the present education system, 'integration' usually has two meanings:

- 'Increasing the participation of students who have a disability into the educational programs and the social life of regular schools.
- Maintaining the participation of all students in the educational programs and social life of regular schools.'[1]

Educational integration means providing services to regular classrooms so that they can meet the needs of both those students who are presently segregated and those students who are at risk of being segregated because of their disability. It means providing appropriate services to a number of educational facilities so that they can each meet the needs of students with a disability. It means providing students with a choice.

Both these aspects of educational integration describe how the process of integration can operate in all communities, not just in education—giving people the chance to move out of segregated communities and giving them the chance to stay in regular communities. However ensuring that integration can happen and does operate in this way is not always straightforward.

THE PRINCIPLES OF INTEGRATION

You certainly can't judge integration by appearances. You can't have a checklist for integration with an item that says 'All teenagers in Op-shop clothes are not integrated into a community' or 'All teenagers in jeans are integrated into a community'. Likewise a disabled student at a special school can't be judged as either 'integrated' or 'not integrated'. It is the range of choices and the choice process behind the decision of 'Op-shop' or 'special school' that are the indicators of integration. The student at the special school may have been given a full range of school choices and the special school provided him with the best opportunities. Integration isn't a matter of appearances or checklists. It is a matter of choices, processes and opportunities rather than a matter of the actual decision made.

Unfortunately there is not an ideal model which can be followed to ensure that integration will 'work', but integration can happen when a community follows certain principles. The following four principles of integration—social justice, equal opportunity, non-categorisation and non-segregation—do not on their own define or describe integration, or even ensure that integration will happen, but they must be followed for integration to be able to happen.

THE NOTION OF SOCIAL JUSTICE

All people have equal value.   Communities should reflect each person's right to an equal share of the services and goods available.

- A council learn-to-swim program that refuses lessons to a person with a physical disability because 'It's a waste of time; he'll never learn to swim properly anyway' is valuing this person less than other people. It is ignoring the right of this person to an equal share of the council's services.
- A drama club that tells a child who has calipers that she can't perform in the end-of-year concert because the costume and props would have to be altered, is not following the notion of social justice. A child with a disability has a right to an equal share of whatever equipment and instructor's time the club has available.

THE RIGHT OF EQUAL OPPORTUNITY

All people have the right to be treated equally.   No person should be discriminated against or be treated less favourably than another; neither should rules or conditions exist in a community that make it more difficult for some people to participate than others.

Equal opportunity should 'fit' everybody

- A company that advertises for a female typist is not acknowledging the right of equal opportunity because it is discriminating against males.
- A clothing shop with fitting rooms that are too small for a wheelchair is not acknowledging the right of equal opportunity because it is discriminating against some people who have physical impairments.
- A children's aerobic class which won't let a blind child join because 'She'll get in the way of other children' is not acknowledging the right of equal opportunity. It is discriminating against the child's right to join the aerobic class.

Equal opportunity allows choices. Real choices can only be made when a person is offered a range of experiences from which to choose. For some people, integration may mean having more choices than were previously available to them, even if the range of choices is not identical to that offered to other people. Certainly most people have some limits on their choices—there are often things that they would like to do but can't, perhaps because of financial or family commitments, or because of lack of skill or talent. Some people have trouble making choices and many people find making risky choices difficult: such as choosing something with which they are unfamiliar, which they feel they may not enjoy, may not succeed at or where they may look foolish. Most people choose not to take up all the opportunities they do have and reject some. They are still making a choice.

Some people have more choices than others (perhaps they have less family commitments, more money or more ability in some areas) and so among all community members there is not absolute equality of opportunity and of choice. However the principle of equal opportunity ensures that a person with a disability is no more restricted in her range of choices than most community members.

- A blind boy who is only offered employment training for doormat weaving, process packaging or as a telephonist is not being offered a range of employment choices.
- A clothing shop assistant who only selects dowdy, matronly clothes for a young girl in a wheelchair is not providing a real choice.

Equal opportunity allows risks to be taken.   Equal opportunity means not only having choices, but also making choices and taking responsibility for the consequences of those choices. It is being allowed to make a risky choice while knowing the risk, acknowledging responsibility for the choice and being dignified in the subsequent success or failure.

Equal opportunity ensures that a person with a disability is offered risky choices (just as other people are) even if he doesn't choose the risky choice initially or make that choice again. He is allowed the dignity of taking risks.

- A parent who doesn't allow a child pickles with her cheese sandwich because 'She won't like them' is not offering the child the dignity of risk.
- A gym class which won't let a person with a physical disability join because 'He'll fall over' is not allowing the person the dignity of risk.
- An employer who doesn't invite one of her employees who has a disability to the staff dinner-dance because 'He'll feel out of place' is not offering him the dignity of risk.

THE PRINCIPLE OF NON-CATEGORISATION

People are individuals.   All people have many things in common and some things that are different. Putting people in categories (categorisation) leads to the idea that everything about all the people in that category is the same. This does not make sense. 'All blonde ladies are secretaries' and 'All people who eat peanut butter are happy' are just as senseless categorisations as 'All disabled children need special schools'. I'm sure some blonde ladies will want to be secretaries, some people are happy to eat peanut butter sandwiches, and some children with a disability choose to get special help with their lessons at special schools. But not all of them.

Non-categorisation ensures that people are treated as individuals and are given a full range of choices.

- A craft co-operative that offers people who are aboriginal only boomerang-making or traditional bark painting is not practising the principle of non-categorisation.

- An employment service that only offers women jobs as typists or shop assistants is not practising the principle of non-categorisation.
- A childcare centre that offers a child with Down syndrome little more than a musical toy or a cuddle ('They're so affectionate and they all love music') is not practising the principle of non-categorisation.

THE OPPORTUNITY FOR NON-SEGREGATION

People need contact with a variety of people.   People need the opportunity to mix with people of varying ages, sexes, abilities and interests. This helps them understand about various ways of life and thus to make a choice about their own way of life with greater self-awareness.

Many people who have a disability have been segregated (grouped and separated from other people). Segregation usually follows categorisation of people (in the context of this book, categorisation as 'disabled'); if people haven't been categorised it is more difficult to segregate them. Depending on the constancy of the segregation, people in a segregated community may be limited in their knowledge and experience of other communities and thus have limited ability to make a choice about how they want to live, work, play or learn.

Segregated communities may have special services and facilities that suit the type of people who are within them; on the other hand they may not provide anything that is especially appropriate and instead merely provide segregation. Some people require special services or facilities (perhaps an assistant or piece of equipment) in order to participate in some aspects of life; some people choose to get these special services at a segregated community because it suits them best. Some special services may only be available at segregated communities. If these same special services were available at ordinary communities as well as at segregated communities, people may prefer to use them in the ordinary communities; at the very least they would have had a choice.

Segregation isn't the opposite of integration. Segregation is about physical separation. Integration is about physical togetherness, but it is also about participation, interaction, interdependence, choices and variety. Attending a special community because it provides a service you want is different to choosing to attend that community from among a range of special and ordinary communities each providing the service you want. Attending a special community because it provides a service you want is also different to attending because you've been categorised and limited to that sort of community only.

Non-segregation implies knowing the enormous variety of choices people can make and do make about their lives.

- A person with a disability who lives in an out-of-town institution surrounded by a high wall is more segregated than a person living on his own, with his family or in a community group home in a suburban street.

- A person with a disability who works in a sheltered workshop with people who have few skills and who communicate poorly is more segregated than a person who works in a factory with people of various ages, sexes, nationalities, skills and opinions.
- A child with a disability who goes to a special school for children with her category of disability—perhaps a school for blind or physically handicapped children—is more segregated than a child who goes to her local school with children at varying stages of development and with a variety of abilities and interests.

Integration means not just being together, but doing activities together. It is not just polite attendance at a community or participation in its activities; it also implies interaction and interdependence between community members. Integration means being part of a community. It is not just having a job, but getting a real wage for real work; it is not just attending the local school with peers, but learning with them; it is not just joining the local scout group, but going on camp and doing duty on carwash day with them; it is not just going to the pub with friends, but shouting a round of drinks.

Integration—chances and choices for everyone.

Chapter Two

WHY INTEGRATE A PERSON WHO HAS A DISABILITY?

The integration of people with a disability into a community reflects a general trend towards social justice for all minority groups—all people have equal value. If people are equally valued then they have the right to be treated equally and to have equal opportunities. Thus, people with a disability should be able to share equally with all people the good, the bad, the easy and the difficult aspects of any community. They should share opportunities for education, free speech and breakfast in bed, but also share transport strikes, economic inflation and the dishwashing.

As well as reflecting social justice, integration is a response to society's re-examination of the validity of past reasons for segregating people who have a disability. Arguments like 'They're happier with their own kind', 'They feel depressed and jealous seeing normal people' and 'Their needs are so special that they need a special place all of their own' are seen now as emotional rationalisations.

Integration is not just about getting people out of segregated communities; neither is it just about getting people into ordinary communities. It is about giving people a choice of communities and a range of opportunities.

Integration stresses abilities not disabilities. It rightly presumes that there is more about a person with a disability that is the same as all other people than there is difference: the same physical characteristics and social needs, the same needs to be challenged, to be cared for, to be respected and to belong. Integration works from a perspective of normality and asks 'Why segregate?', whereas segregation sometimes works from a perspective of differences and asks 'Why integrate?'. By working from a perspective of normality, integration asks 'Are there some special services this person needs? Are they available in a variety of communities or only in a segregated community?'

Some people with a disability find that in a segregated community they have people who understand them, equipment they need and schooling or work geared to their individual abilities and difficulties; they receive good care and have a sense of security and belonging. Hopefully these people use a segregated community because it best meets their needs, not because they were 'categorised' into it, because it was the only community that they considered, or because it was the only community which had the special services they needed.

In some segregated communities a person with a disability can certainly receive good care but she may learn other things, too: to be dependent on other people, not to question her life or make choices about it. In this instance a person may lose her individuality and take little responsibility for her actions.

Many people believe that ordinary communities are able to provide care and programs that meet the individual needs of people with a disability just as appropriately as do the care and programs at segregated communities. Additionally, they believe that integration can overcome many of the disadvantages of segregation and offers additional advantages to people with a disability and to other community members.

THE BENEFITS OF INTEGRATION FOR A PERSON WITH A DISABILITY

Integration provides ordinary peer models. People learn many things from watching and interacting with other people: how to kick a football, wait a turn in a conversation, play chess, make a sandwich, put on a 'Bandaid', ask for help or make a complaint.

> *A parent:* Jane is usually so slow to get going in the mornings, but when her older cousin came to stay and shared her room, she was up, dressed and breakfasted in no time at all. She just did it on her own in order to keep up with her cousin, and we didn't have to nag and remind her at all.

If people learn from other people around them, then being with a broad range of people doing a broad range of activities (non-segregation) is important. Segregation can limit the opportunity for people with a disability to learn normal activities and behaviour from peer modelling because the people around them (in the segregated community) may not behave and participate in activities in ordinary ways.

People in a segregated community may learn other things from the people around them: perhaps how to yell for attention, how to spill a drink at the table and how to throw toys. If these are things that the other people in their community do (intentionally or not), if this is the behaviour a person sees most often, then this is the behaviour he will learn most easily.

Integration provides the opportunity for people with a disability to be with people who don't have a disability so that the behaviour and language most likely to be copied is ordinary behaviour and language.

Integration provides functional learning. People learn skills most easily in real situations as the need arises (functional learning). Integration not only offers community members the ability to learn a large range of skills through peer modelling, but also to learn them in a natural way—to learn them from ordinary people (Dad, a neighbour, a shopkeeper) in ordinary settings (a backyard, next door, a shop).

Some of these skills could be taught at a segregated community but they would be taught by only a few people (caregivers) and often in isolated ways where it is hard to see their relevance. Learning skills in an ordinary community (natural learning) provides a reason, motivation and interactions which are likely to make more sense than learning in a segregated community.

Behaviours and expectations in a segregated community may differ from those of a regular community. These different expectations may have been established for good reasons (like allowing for individual differences between people) but they may make it more difficult for a person to move from a segregated to a regular community. Additionally, some skills can seem meaningless in a segregated community even though they will be vital in a regular community. Why learn to wait your turn in a conversation when other people often interrupt you and very few of your peers speak anyway? Why learn to make a sandwich if your meals are provided for you and so you have no reason to make a sandwich? Why learn how to ask for help when help is given if you've asked for it or not, if you want it or not and if you need it or not?

Learning is a means to an end, to prepare people for the real world. Functional learning understands this. When a child with a disability walks to the local school she is getting real-life experience of the skills she needs: road safety, being on time and remembering directions. These skills could be taught at a segregated special school in special ways, but the child is more likely to use them spontaneously walking to a regular school because they are needed and they make sense. By using them in such a natural way the child may better understand their usefulness in many communities (not just in the community where they were taught), and she may use them more often than if she had been taught them in a classroom with a pretend road.

Integration provides more chances, choices and variety.   Life can be rich and diverse. Integration gives a person with a disability the chance to experience the richness and diversity of many communities: living in different countries and housing arrangements, eating and working in different places, liking and disliking a variety of people. It can give a person with a disability experiences and knowledge to make real choices.

Segregation, by limiting this experience and knowledge, may lead to a secondary handicap, another disadvantage on top of a person's disability: a restriction of the person's choices and learning opportunities. Similarly, the limited social opportunities and expectations of some segregated communities restrict a person's social experiences and thus can confine his social development.

Learning is not just an academic experience, it is the continuous process by which people learn to cope with the various communities to which they belong. If they experience very few environments—if they live in a small farm community, among a family of twelve children or at an institution for disabled people—then it may be difficult for them to learn to live in another environment—in a large metropolitan area, on their own or with a group of people who don't have a disability.

Friends that children make while they are young are often life-long friends and form a pool from which future contacts are made. Limiting a

Choices: people are individuals

child's contacts to a small group of people who also have a disability may thus also limit his later opportunities in life; it may limit the opportunities to have friends without a disability and to join in the richness and diversity of their lives.

Integration is reality.   Isn't integration the natural way to live? Isn't it natural to have choices, to mix with a wide range of people? Isn't it natural to go to school with local children whose abilities and interests are diverse; to work, shop and pray with a variety of people? Isn't it natural to meet people at work who are different to those with whom you live or socialise? These are things which most people do, or have the opportunity to do. So it may be segregation, and not integration, which needs to be justified.

Integration can provide a person with an environment that lets him discover what he can do, what he can learn and what he can't do. Integration can thus provide him with reality: the good and the bad of any situation, the risks and the consequences. In an ordinary community a person with a disability may find that his disability is sometimes more of a handicap (a disadvantage) than in a segregated community. Though the opportunities of an ordinary community may expand his choices, people's attitudes and architectural barriers may likewise limit his choices. This is the reality of life, that things will not always be ideal.

For a person with a disability, integration may be the only way to provide this sense of reality—of good, bad and compromise—as segregation may have protected her from the things she can't do or doesn't know. Integration lets her experience the natural consequences of her disability. Integration can provide a person with a realistic sense of self-worth. With help, integration can give a person the opportunity to see where she stands in relation to other people, to value the things she does well and to keep in perspective the things she can't do or finds more difficult.

NORMALISATION

The advantages of integration for a person with a disability (peer modelling, functional learning, chances, choices, variety and reality) are outcomes of the *theory of normalisation*—'Making available to all persons with disabilities or other handicaps, patterns of life and conditions of everyday living which are as close as possible to, or indeed the same as, the regular circumstances and way of life of society'.[2]

Normalisation is concerned with the idea of *social value* and in some countries it is called 'social role valorisation' in order to stress this. It aims to restore the value of equality to people who have a disability. It does this by providing a framework to help people develop skills and a social image, both of which will be valued. In the past people with a disability were often treated with little value—put in large, remote, segregated institutions, denied education and compared with animals and vegetables. Normalisation is a theory that aims to redress these past discriminations; it applies social justice to all people and helps them be valued equally.

Normalisation does not aim to make people 'normal', 'average' or 'identical' or make them do what most people do. It works at changing environments, not people. Normalisation recognises that people are individual and that their lifestyles and choices will vary.

> Normalisation does not mean that if a person prefers a shower to a bath and you know the majority of people prefer baths, that you introduce a behaviour modification program to encourage baths and to discourage showers. It does not mean that because you have never seen a child pick his nose, yet you know that most children pick their nose from time to time, that you show him how you pick your nose and co-actively help him to pick his.[3]

One of the most effective ways to implement the theory of normalisation is to follow the principles of integration: social justice, equal opportunity, non-categorisation and non-segregation. Following these principles will make the environment more normal, will give people with a disability a more normal 'pattern of life and conditions of everyday living'.

THE BENEFITS OF INTEGRATION FOR A COMMUNITY

Integration provides diverse communities. Community members are entitled to communities of genuine diversity. They should have the chance to live, work, learn and play with a variety of people including people with and without a disability. Integration provides teachers with a class of students which reflects the genuine diversity of the community; it offers students a group whose members will be as varied in abilities as the people they will meet when they are adults. It provides manufacturers and shopkeepers contact with the diverse community for whom they produce and sell goods.

Integration offers families a sense of being a normal family unit: the opportunity to have all their children at the one school, to have their child's school and thus her playmates nearby, to only have 'parent-teacher nights', 'hot cross bun sales' and 'working bees' at one school. In fact integration can overcome many of the disadvantages that a child with a disability can bring to a family. Certainly integration can overcome the disadvantages to the family that segregation can bring.

Integration provides community education.   If people without a disability are to function responsibly in a diverse society, their education must introduce them to the diverse representation of people within that society. Integration offers community members the opportunity to gain increased understanding of the needs and abilities of other people in a way that may never be gained elsewhere—certainly not through textbooks or 'disability awareness activities'.

Education involves developing not only particular skills, but also human qualities: the ability to live with and understand (though not necessarily agree with) other people. Being a human being means not only having contact with other people, but also having reciprocal relationships, being interdependent. Integration can thus help all community members in their growth, learning and development.

When a person with a disability is integrated into a community, it gives community members the opportunity to know that person well, to learn of his habits, likes and dislikes that are unrelated to his disability; people get to know him as an individual. It discourages the notion of two groups of people—normal and abnormal—and reduces the risk of categorisation. It helps dissolve the values and assumptions which are attached to people with a disability.

Integration allows community members to understand the individuality and also the ordinariness of people with a disability. It allows the person with the disability to experience the variety of other people's choices. Integration is a cornerstone which develops a group of people into a true community; it provides them with a real education on the rights and responsibilities of being community members.

Chapter Three

HOW DOES INTEGRATION HAPPEN?

Integration means not just being together but doing activities together. It is not just polite attendance at a community or participation in its activities; it also implies interaction and interdependence between community members. Integration means being part of a community, belonging to the community.

Integration 'works' when four different aspects of community functioning are fulfilled. Integration can begin to happen when a person with a disability **attends** a regular community. However simply being together doesn't necessarily lead to participation and interaction of any sort, let alone acceptance, co-operation or interdependence. On the other hand, you can't interact unless you are together.

Integration starts to happen when a person with a disability not only attends a regular community, but **participates** in the community's programs and uses its resources—when her chances and choices at the community are equal to those of other community members.

Integration is happening when a person with a disability not only participates in the community's programs, but also in its social activities—when he **interacts** with other community members. The best resources, facilities and programs can provide choices but only community members can provide a sense of 'belonging'.

Integration works best when community members not only interact with each other but are **interdependent**—when they each give and take something from the community, when they each depend on and help other community members.

Well, how does integration happen? How does a person with a disability attend and participate, interact and interdepend, belong and become accepted? If only there were a simple answer! Unfortunately there is no foolproof scale model, diagram or checklist of how to successfully integrate people with a disability into a community; neither does integration follow directly from rules, regulations or laws.

Integration is hard enough to define, but it is just as difficult to describe how integration happens and to ensure that it does happen. However, by following some processes a community can show its understanding and implementation of the principles of integration. The more that these formal and social processes of integration are followed, the more real will integration be.

Before describing either the formal or the social processes that help integration happen, it is necessary to describe a process that stops integration happening and has led in the past to the segregation of people with a disability.

DIFFERENCES AND DEVIANCE

Segregation is based on the notion of deviance; deviance is based on categorisation. Deviance is the categorisation of a minority group of people based on a 'difference' (perhaps 'alcoholics', 'ethnics', 'people with a disability'). This minority group is sufficiently different to be outside the main category ('normal'); the difference is important and undesirable and so the people with this difference are labelled 'deviant'.

It is only if a difference is socially important and seen as undesirable (negatively valued) that people are labelled deviant. A person who doesn't own a television is seen as different but not deviant because owning a television is not seen as socially important. An Australian adult who goes barefoot is seen as different but not deviant. Similarly, great intelligence or beauty does not lead to a label of 'deviant' because beauty and intelligence are positively valued, desirable. The degree of difference often influences whether a person is perceived as 'deviant'. A fat person may be only 'different', but a very obese person may be different enough to be seen as 'deviant'.

Over time society has changed its attitudes towards various types of social groups, often through altering its perception of what is 'deviant' and of what is merely 'different'; single parents, homosexuals, adopted children and divorcees were all seen as more deviant twenty years ago than they are now. Voting rights are now extended to Aborigines and non-landowners. Similarly what previously would have been regarded as 'different' may become 'deviant', for example the concept of 'normal weight' seems to have shifted—what was once seen as plump but healthy is now seen as self-indulgent and unhealthy. It is undesirable and so has become 'deviant' rather than 'different'.

Of course, even people labelled 'deviant' are 'normal' in a lot more ways than they are 'different'—they are humans, they go to sleep at night, perhaps they go to the football, read a book or eat pies and chips occasionally—even if they also have a disability or are obese.

Deviance is not a characteristic of the individual who has been labelled 'deviant'— it is only a social judgement. A fat person or a person with a disability is not in himself deviant, but particular aspects of himself (his weight or his disability) have caused other people to judge him as different enough to be deviant. Deviance is a judgement by one powerful group on another group who do not have the same values and qualities as the original powerful group. Deviance is a perceptual definition which allows a majority group to see itself as more able and more powerful.

Because deviance is based on categorisation it can lead to the segregation of people in those categories. Over time, these segregated people can become discriminated against not just because they are different, but because they have been segregated for so long that their differences are now uncommon in 'normal' communities—in everyday communities—and are seen as negative, as odd, as deviant.

So integration can only happen when categorisation is removed so that people cannot be categorised, cannot be judged as deviant and cannot then be segregated.

THE FORMAL PROCESSES OF INTEGRATION: ATTENDANCE AND PARTICIPATION

Integration can be helped to happen in formal ways when particular laws or policies (like the Equal Opportunity Act or a school policy on integration) are developed into guiding principles and followed by the community. Such formal processes particularly help the 'attendance' and 'participation' aspects of integration. However formal processes alone will not ensure that integration happens; formal processes can't ensure interaction and interdependence between community members.

All of a community's policies reflect its attitudes. Each of a community's written or unwritten laws, policies, guidelines or principles should be based on the principles of social justice—all people have equal value. This will ensure that the principles of integration—social justice, equal opportunity, non-categorisation and non-segregation—are also followed.

Some communities feel the need for a specific integration policy. Developing such a policy may be useful, but legislating for the rights of one group of people may only harden existing prejudices and create negative attitudes. To avoid this, an integration policy needs to be seen as a specific example of the community's wider policies. It is not 'favouritism for people with a disability' but an example of how social justice can be applied to particular community members.

The formal processes of integration can be implemented irrespective of whether a community has an integration policy. Each of its policies can reflect attitudes that understand the needs of all community members including those members who have a disability. (Each of these planning principles is expanded in chapter 6):

- Overall community goals reflect social justice.
- Community members are not categorised.
- Community members are not segregated.
- Community members have equal opportunities.
- Community members have choices.
- Community members are allowed to take risks.
- The least restrictive environment is available.

The community may specifically address the needs of its members who have a disability by developing a community plan for integration or an integration policy. This policy should reflect not only the social justice that underlies all of the community's policies, but also additional factors that relate to the specific social justice issue of integration:

- Overall community goals for integration are needed.
- Integration is ongoing.
- Integration means participation, interaction and interdependence.
- Plans to reach the overall goals are needed.
- The community's existing resources are used.
- Additional resources may be required.
- Staff and community preparation for and education about integration may be needed.
- Each person with a disability requires an individual integration program.
- A community's plan for integration must be reviewed.

THE SOCIAL PROCESSES OF INTEGRATION: INTERACTION AND INTERDEPENDENCE

As well as through formal processes, integration can be helped to happen in informal ways: when a person with a disability plays on the beach, has a drink at the bar, chats at the bus stop, plays cards with a club, goes to a party or argues with a friend.

However neither bringing people together through a formal policy nor informally doing activities together ensures that integration is really happening; neither process ensures that a person with a disability is equally involved in the jokes, the social life, the gossip and the opportunities of the schoolplace, workplace or recreation community. Both formal policies and informal contacts need to be supported by the right attitudes to make integration work.

Integration is heavily influenced by the attitudes both of individual people in a community and of the media. The social processes of 'attitudes' provide the interaction and interdependence to the attendance and participation provided by the formal processes of 'policies'. Particular attitudes, preferably accompanied by particular formal processes, make integration most likely to happen.

THE DEVELOPMENT OF ATTITUDES

People's attidudes are developed by social processes, and are influenced by the attitudes of both other community members and of the media, and through personal experience. Changing people's attitudes on any topic is notoriously difficult—try changing someone else's political or religious views and you'll know what I mean! The difficulty lies in the fact that there is an enormous difference between obtaining factual information and acting on it, and between actually believing the information and acting according to the belief (rather than just doing what you are told is right).

However over time society has changed its attitudes towards various social groups, including its attitude towards people who have a disability and towards their integration into community activities. Before the 1940s, all students who were not 'ineducable' were educated together no matter their ability level. In the 1950s there was a swing towards special education: special schools, classes and teachers. In the 1980s there has been a swing back towards the notion of all students being educated together in one integrated education system. Attitudes have changed!

During any period there are always some people who are more tolerant of differences than others—in the Tate Gallery in London is an old family portrait which includes a child with Down syndrome. This was painted in an era when disability was usually hidden, yet this family went against the social pressures of the day and included him in their family portrait and presumably in their lives.

Attitudes are influenced by the example of other people.   People's attitudes are more likely to change when the attitudes of people around them change. People learn from attitudes around them, just like children learn from peer modelling (chapter 2). So each person in a community can start to change the attitude of the whole community by changing her own attitude. She can show her own positive attitude towards integration and positively influence other people's attitudes. When people's behaviour shows their acceptance of the social justice of integrating people with a disability into their community then other community members and other communities will gradually become more accepting, too.

Attitudes are influenced by experiences.   Personal experiences have a powerful influence on attitudes and opinions. Direct, personal contacts with a person who has a disability provide a powerful influence on people's attitudes towards integration.

Contact with people who have a disability will not on its own lead to acceptance of them, but the right sorts of contacts will certainly assist such acceptance. Community members learn something about people who have a disability when they see ramps at the shops or sign-language used on T.V., when they hear an audible traffic-light signal or when they see a wheelchair-access telephone cubicle. These adaptations and facilities indicate that people with a disability do go to the shops, watch T.V., walk across roads and use telephones—activities that some people may have thought people with a disability never did. Community members learn even more about people who have a disability when they actually see them shopping, crossing the road or using the telephone—when they see them participating in the community, involved with the community's facilities and resources.

Community members learn even more again when they see people with a disability not only doing mundane things like shopping, crossing the road or using a telephone, but also doing 'clever' things like working or going to school; 'fun' things like dancing, playing football or putting a bet on the races; 'exotic' things like running a marathon, making a lot of money or travelling overseas.

Community members learn most when they actually shop, cross the road, go to school, work or play football with people who have a disability—when they interact and are interdependent with them. Such real-life interdependence is more important in the development of a positive attitude towards integration than the example of other people's attitudes or than 'education' about disability. 'Disability awareness activities' (chapter 7) have their place, but ongoing appropriate involvement and interaction with people who have a disability is more effective.

Particular types of involvement and interaction, especially situations of interdependence, are more likely to produce positive attitudes towards people who have a disability. The organisation of such situations is a practical process that is covered in chapter 11.

Attitudes are influenced by the example of the media. Many community attitudes are influenced by media items in books, films, television, newspapers and magazines. The media affects people by example, but leaves them (hopefully) to agree or disagree, to question and to re-evaluate their opinions (on integration and on any other issue). However the media are a powerful source of influence and by repetition can affect opinions. If people see or hear an attitude that is different to their own more often than they take time to reaffirm their own attitude, then they can be easily influenced to change. That is the power of the media.

The media heavily influences community attitudes towards people with a disability. Unfortunately in Australia, people with a disability are not often portrayed in the media with much reality, as ordinary people in ordinary situations. How long is it since you've seen an advertisement including a person who not only has a disability but also owns the best car, wears the right clothes, has the freshest mouth, uses the right margarine, washes with the best soap powder or is seen at the newest restaurant? For that matter, how long since you've seen an advertisement including a person with a disability at all, even a person with a disability who uses the wrong soap powder or deodorant, or is the one with the lank, dull hair, the beer pot or indigestion? Advertisements have very little to do with reality, with the everyday lives of most people, but they are even less representative of the lives of people with a disability.

When people with a disability *are* portrayed in the media, usually in literature and film, they are often portrayed as 'bad' people who get their just deserts, with their disability being an outward sign of an inner evil: Captain Hook, the Hunchback of Notre Dame. Alternatively they may be portrayed as 'good' people who have made great achievements against all odds—'Blind girl passes exams'. Villainous heroes sometimes pretend they have a disability (can't see, are in a wheelchair or have a limp) in order to steal, to win, to gain sympathy or to be noticed by the gorgeous girl.

When the media portrays people with a disability in these ways it projects a sensational image and avoids the real issues of many people with a disability: segregation, discrimination and lack of access. By glossing over the problem of having a disability ('Ironside' in an environment

What's 'normal'? What's 'average'? What's 'success'?

that eternally has wheelchair access) these media images do not contribute to real community acceptance.

Another area of media attention is charity fundraising. Such attention often does a disservice towards people who have a disability, since public promotion may present people with a disability as childlike, invariably as 'cute', and rarely as severely or multiply disabled. Because disabled people are presented only for fundraising purposes they may become labelled in people's minds as 'poor unfortunates' who are in need of public sympathy.

The money raised from fundraising may go to large city institutions; this means that people with a disability who wish to use these services may need to leave their own communities. Irrespective of how the funds are raised and used, donors and fundraisers can also be working at grassroots level in their own communities. Positive, accepting attitudes provide opportunities for local people with a disability to be integrated into their own local communities.

ATTITUDES THAT SUPPORT INTEGRATION

The attitudes of a community are demonstrated in both its formal policies and procedures and in its members' informal social interactions. Both

Categorisation is a powerful influence

these processes can help integration by supporting its principles; equally they can hinder integration by rejecting its principles. Thus the attitudes of community members influence integration's outcome, irrespective of how well the community's formal processes are designed. Community members will become more accepting of people who have a disability and of integration when the words and actions around them—of individual people and of the media—support integration.

Attitudes that support integration need not be obviously different to many other community attitudes. They can be low-key attitudes; they can become habits below community consciousness. They can let integration become part of the background of a community, rather than a foreground issue.

An attitude of non-categorisation supports integration.   Some people with a disability perceive themselves as incompetent, a perception established in their childhood and subsequently reinforced by labelling, diagnosis and categorisation. If people do not label a person with a disability, it is harder for him to label himself.

> I know a child with cerebral palsy who didn't line up in either the 'boys' or the 'girls' line at the local store to get a present from Father Christmas. When asked why, she said she was a 'chair' and Father Christmas didn't have a line for 'chairs'. At her school which is for physically handicapped children, she had always been in the line for 'chairs', for wheelchairs (that is, 'Boys over there, girls up there and "chairs" over here').

The media can show an attitude of non-categorisation—not 'Spastic girl writes book' but 'Woman writes book' or, if appropriate, 'Personal experience adds authority to book'.

If people aren't labelled and categorised it is harder to make snap judgements about them. If people aren't thought of as alike, they won't be treated as alike. They will be treated as individuals who have various likes, dislikes, habits, jobs, schools, pets, houses and, Oh yes, they also have a disability. They will be integrated into their community.

An attitude of non-segregation supports integration. Community members' attitudes can categorise people according to their differences and then segregate them, or can respect people's individual abilities and contributions and integrate them into the community. The media can also show an attitude of non-segregation—not 'Retarded people grow carrots on their own farm' but 'Bumper carrot crop'.

An attitude recognising people's rights supports integration. A person with a disability has the same rights as other people—the right to expect respect, to be given appropriate privacy, to be allowed to take risks, to choose friends and to refuse to be patronised. If individual people and the media frequently asked themselves 'How would I treat this person if they didn't have a disability?', then real integration would be encouraged.

An attitude of acceptance of people's individuality supports integration. People with a disability, just like all people, are individuals. All people have many things in common and some things that are different. When other people recognise and respect this individuality as being human, as being the same individuality that any person in a group can show, then real integration is encouraged.

- A blind person may wear loud coloured clothes not because 'She's blind and doesn't know how to match her wardrobe, poor thing'. She may choose to be a flamboyant dresser.
- A person in a wheelchair may have an untidy house not because 'He can't do it all, you know'. He may just not choose to value a tidy house.

An attitude of respect for disability supports integration. Having a disability is a way of life for people who are disabled. It is important not to ignore their disability, because this would ignore part of their individuality, their culture and their self-concept. A Japanese person who comes to live in Australia will be influenced by her earlier learning and experiences in Japan and other people understand this. A country boy who comes to live in a capital city will be influenced by his country environment and upbringing; it will not be ignored by other people—it is part of him. A person with a disability will also be influenced by how her disability has altered her learning and experiences—it must be accepted as part of herself.

Integration implies acceptance of a person and his disability—not making him the same, but assimilating his way of life and his individuality into a community whose members have many ways of life.

An attitude that allows people to take responsibility for their decisions understands integration. People with a disability deserve the same treatment as people without a disability. They deserve the same rights, but must accept the same responsibilities, too. Being part of a community—learning, contributing and sharing—should be no more difficult for a person with a disability than for other people, presuming that she has been exposed to and modelled by the same very normal shaping influences as have other people. Unfortunately this is not always the case. In subtle and not so subtle ways people have probably reacted differently to the things that she has said or done: allowed behaviours they wouldn't accept from other people, denied her opportunities because 'She wouldn't understand', ignored her attempts to join in or isolated her from the natural consequences of her behaviour. No matter how hard some people try to 'treat her normally' other people often react in different ways, at different intensities or with inconsistencies to a person who has a disability.

People with a disability deserve to be informed of their mistakes, not 'Don't worry, he doesn't know any better'; they deserve to be punished for their offences, not 'I won't give him a speeding ticket, he's a paraplegic driver'; they deserve to compete equally, not 'I'll give him the winner's ribbon because he tried hard'; they deserve to conform to the rules, not 'I'll make allowances, he won't do it again'.

By providing a person who has a disability with consistent natural consequences to his behaviour, his understanding of and responsibility for consequences will be encouraged, and thus real integration will be enhanced.

Integration happens primarily when people's attitudes let it happen. Attitudes add the humanity—the individuality, belonging and acceptance—to the mechanics that legislation, guiding principles and interaction can provide. Formal processes can ensure community attendance and participation for a person who has a disability; but his participation is given quality by the interaction and interdependence that develops through the attitudes of community members. People make integration happen, make integration as natural, right and as effective as it can be; individual people make integration work.

Chapter Four

PERSPECTIVES

People are individual; communities are composed of a number of individuals, each bringing opinions, feelings, fears, hopes and prejudices to any situation. People's feelings, thoughts and reactions towards integration will thus be varied. Their feelings may be influenced by the role they play in the process (parent, staff, community member or person with a disability), and by their experience of and knowledge about integration. Some people have an opinion about integration despite having no role in it, no experience and little knowledge about it. Such 'armchair observer' opinions are common in relation to topical issues like integration, but it is important to recognise and separate 'inexperienced' opinions from the opinions of people more closely involved with integration.

Humans are individuals and are fallible; their feelings, thoughts and reactions to any situation are neither predictable nor constant. People involved with integration are human and so their feelings may fluctuate, change and even surprise them. Certainly no two people will have identical feelings, opinions and commitments towards integration. However if they have the same role in the integration process, if they share the same perspective of it, their opinions and feelings may be similar.

THE PARENTS' PERSPECTIVE

Parents' reactions, opinions and commitment to the integration of their child into community activities vary enormously: from parent to parent, from day to day, from situation to situation. Also, many parents have mixed feelings about integration:

> I feel John gets the opportunities at regular school, but I pay the price. It's damn hard for me. If John was at special school it would be easier for me—I'd just be one of the Mums—but John would pay the price.

Parents' opinions are no doubt influenced by their current involvement (or not) with integration, and by the various reasons that have led them to consider integrating their child into community activities.

Parents may not want their child to be more integrated. Some parents feel that they and their child are well served by the segregated community she currently attends; they are not seeking any further integra-

27

tion. (When they say they are not interested in integration, they are usually thinking 'integrated into school Y or community X' as most children are well integrated into an important aspect of community life anyway—integrated into their families.)

> School is one part of her life and it is a special school, but Jane lives at home with us and that is integration too.

Some parents may not want their child to be integrated into a particular community, but feel they have no choice: they may be geographically isolated with no segregated community; they may feel pushed into integration by other people who 'know best' or their spouse may support and implement integration for their child, despite their own differing opinion.

Parents may doubt the value of integration.   Some parents have significant doubts about integration for their child but perhaps see the particular segregated community alternative that is available as even more doubtful. They may see integration as the best of a poor range of options.

Parents may carefully consider integration.   Some parents have carefully considered many of the arguments for and against integration, and support it for their child in this community at this time, but not necessarily in other communities or at other times. Their belief in the value of integration—the 'rightness' of integration—may vary between different communities: perhaps integration at computer club but not school, school but not school camp, paid childcare centre but not voluntary playgroup.

Parents may totally support integration.   Some parents have never considered anything other than integration and see it as the natural course of events.

PARENTS' FEELINGS ABOUT INTEGRATION

A list of feelings common to all parents who have a child with a disability could never be finalised—the parents differ, the children differ, the disabilities are varied, different situations produce different feelings, and parents' feelings alter over time. Even the two parents of the same child will have different feelings.

Whilst parents' feelings about their child's integration into community activities can vary many feelings are remarkably common to all parents despite differences in their children's abilities and difficulties, and differences in the communities under consideration.

Parents may feel anxious for their child.   Many parents worry that their child will be seen as different and be at risk for verbal, physical or sexual abuse because of this difference. They worry that her self-esteem will drop because of discrimination against her and that she will be left out. They worry that she won't understand what's happening, won't learn in a regular community and that other people won't understand her.

Parents may feel anxious for themselves. Many parents of children with a disability feel different, isolated and out-of-place when their child is integrated into a regular community.

> It is hard to be the parent of the child seen as different when all the other children are seen as similar.

Many parents feel as though all the other parents know each other, have a strong sense of belonging and a right to be there, but that they are only there through charity. They feel obvious and exposed; they feel other people notice them more, stare and wait for them to take the lead. They feel on show; they feel everyone knows them and they have no privacy. They feel they are never a regular parent, never just part of the crowd, and some parents feel they never will be.

Many parents feel they are continually being judged and they often feel devalued—a failure as a parent. Parents may be risking a lot by integrating their child—a normal well behaved child is often a symbol by which other people judge how 'alright' the parents are and by which parents judge themselves. Integration makes many parents face a daily reminder of how different their child is and some parents feel that they share the stigma of being different with their child. They feel other people judge a 'different' child to have a 'different' family and that they aren't accepted or respected by other parents because of this.

> People seem to like healthy, normal, attractive people and John can't be like that. I can't be like that and I can't make our family like that.

Many parents feel confused and uncertain. The rules that apply to other parents seem not to apply to them. They feel unsure when to act and when to let things pass, whether to take the lead and invite other children home or wait to be asked. They feel unsure when to tell people about their child's disability.

> Too much too soon and other people think I am obsessed with him; too little too late and they think I don't want to talk about it.

Parents may feel anxious about other people and their opinions. Parents may worry about what other people will think of them and their child.

> Should I join the babysitting club? Would people expect to get paid more credit hours to babysit my child because he has a disability?

> I invite a child around for Jane to play with and the child comes and then I worry. Did the parent only let the child come because she felt she should? Should I have let her make the first move?

Some parents worry that other people not only see them as 'different', but also as 'pushy'.

> It's not my fault I know more about this place than they do. I had to fight bloody hard to get John in here so of course I know the ins and outs. But they think I'm a know-all.

Some parents worry that their child is used as the scapegoat for any problem that the group has: bad habits in other children, group unrest, missing money or staff exhaustion.

Parents are often concerned about the effect of integration on other members of their family, particularly their other children. If the goal of child-rearing is 'coping with day to day events in ways that will enhance rather than hinder family members' growth and development'[4], then many parents quite rightly take a broad perspective of integration; they may worry about 'the right decision for everyone'.

Parents may feel pressured.   It is reasonable that parents feel pressured when they're also feeling different, isolated, exposed, devalued, confused and worried; the pressure can be immense. Many parents feel overloaded with the job of keeping everyone happy and not upsetting anyone, yet believe that much of the responsibility for their child's successful integration falls on them.

Many parents feel pressure to be a 'good' parent. They feel staff and other parents certainly won't allow them to avoid fundraising, tuckshop or transport duties; what's more, parents often feel pressure to be grateful for the opportunity to participate at all, even if it is in fundraising.

Some parents feel their child is only in an integrated setting temporarily or through charity; they mustn't rock the boat. They feel obligated not to complain about anything: policies, decisions or even if their child is abused. Some parents even feel responsible for the discomfort their child causes other people. They may spend time doing extra tasks to make integration work but feel they have to make all this extra effort look normal, natural, easy.

Some parents pressure themselves to be a good parent in order to compensate for the inconvenience and difficulty that they feel their child causes other people. They may add even more pressure to themselves.

> If they're all going to watch what I do and how I look and what I say just because John's my son, I don't want them to also think I'm fat.

Parents may feel on trial or that their child's integration is a test case. Some parents feel that the future of integration at this community (for their child and any other children) will be judged on this test case.

Parents may feel pleasure and relief.   Many parents feel pride (at least at times) that their child is in a regular community. They feel that they do belong, that they are valued, that their child is secure. They may feel that integration affirms how essentially normal their child is.

> It is lovely being the parent of the child who wins the sack race, even if it is because his legs are so short that he doesn't have to shorten his stride.

They may feel accepted as a family because their child is accepted in a regular community. They may feel a sense of reward for their efforts, for their work over the years with and for their child, and perhaps for their more recent efforts in negotiating her place in the regular community.

They may feel hope that integration will not only offer their child the widest chances and choices in life, but also that his integration will contribute to people's understanding of people with a disability and to their support for integration.

Parents may feel very wary. Many parents can balance their worries against their pride, relief and their hopes for integration, but they are still wary. They may be wary because they have been let down before by promises of services and supports that are in reality less than claimed. They are wary of their child being 'dumped' in a regular community without planning, without support and without the understanding of that community. Many parents feel that they can never rest easily.

I wake up in the morning and think 'What will go wrong today?'

They feel that in a regular community no-one really understands how they feel and no-one wants to know. They may feel loathe to contact special services staff at segregated communities for help because they feel that having rejected a segregated community they will only be seen as 'losers' or 'users' if they now turn around and ask for their help. They feel that there is no-one to help them with decisions. They are wary that integration is a golden rainbow with lots of current attractions, but that at the other end of the rainbow is a bag full of difficult future decisions that must be made alone.

Many parents believe that their child's best chance for long-term satisfaction, for long-term security and acceptance is his ability to fit into society, to demand as little extra as possible from society and hopefully return something to it. Most parents would risk a lot themselves to achieve that for their child. Like all parents, parents of children with a disability want the best for their child; many parents, while recognising the difficulties, believe that integration is that 'best'.

THE STAFF PERSPECTIVE

Many staff members will be involved in integration one way or another. They may be directly responsible for a person with a disability or be a support for staff colleagues who are more directly involved; regardless, they are a member of the community where they work.

Just as the parents of people with a disability have various opinions about integration, the staff—the teachers, sporting coaches and choir masters—also have varying opinions.

Staff may want nothing to do with integration. Some staff believe that segregation (and perhaps even Siberia!) are the best way to deal with society's minority groups, that people with a disability are best put away and forgotten. Other staff may likewise want nothing to do with integration, but they may be slightly more humane. They may recognise that people with a disability exist and have needs, but believe that they are being looked after well 'out there' somewhere.

Staff may acknowledge the value of integration.   Some staff support the underlying social justice of integration and the opportunities and advantages that integration can offer a person with a disability. However these staff may also feel that it is a job for someone else, not for them. They may believe that integration should happen but also know that they don't want to play a part in it. They may know other staff who always 'manage these things well' and 'know just what to do'.

Staff may want to be involved in integration.   Some staff believe that they have a role to play in integration and want to be involved. They recognise the social justice of integration, believe in its positive outcomes and want to take responsibility for their part in making integration work.

STAFF FEELINGS ABOUT INTEGRATION

Staff feelings towards integration, just like parents' feelings, may change over time and vary according to the person whom they are considering.

Staff may feel afraid.   Some staff fears are unfounded, based on lack of knowledge; they can be easily overcome by factual information. These fears often relate to the personal safety of either people with a disability or the other people around them: 'Blind people bump into things', 'Retarded people are aggressive' or 'Epileptics bite their tongues'.

Other fears are based on organisational factors, like fears that the resources needed will disappear once the person's attendance has begun.

> Visiting special education staff? They're like rats on the run once things are up and running.

> A change of government and it will all be down the tube.

Staff may fear that their own usual support mechanisms will not be as helpful as usual; other staff members may have already expressed a lack of belief in integration or may not have enough knowledge and experience about integration to offer support by sharing ideas as they usually do.

Staff may feel unfamiliar and uncertain.   Staff may be unfamiliar with the particular disability and the implications it has had and will continue to have on the person's development. Staff may not know what multiple sclerosis, Down syndrome or spina bifida is, and their unfamiliarity leaves them feeling uncertain of their ability to manage. In time they will realise that it is this particular person with multiple sclerosis or this particular child with Down syndrome that they need to know about, but initially they may not realise that.

Staff may feel uncertain about their role—whether their training and skills are sufficient to manage not only the needs of this person, but also the complementary needs of the other people in the community.

> How much time will it take?

> What will the other people think of Jane?

I have no idea how John will do tests.

What will I say to the other kids and parents? Some of them are already mumbling about how much time Jane is taking up and I am worried about that too.

I don't know where to start.

Staff may feel uncomfortable.   Staff may always have found meetings difficult, but now seem to be having more of them! They may feel uncomfortable with another adult (perhaps an integration assistant) in the room. They may feel uncomfortable trying to balance what they see as their moral responsibility (to take this person into their group) against their fears about their competency. Alternatively they may feel uncomfortable trying to balance their union and legal responsibilities ('You can't take this person until resources and safeguards are guaranteed in writing') against their belief in what integration could offer this person.

Staff may also feel uncomfortable when they consider what other people will think of them. Of course lots of people will admire them tremendously, but some staff may worry that they will look foolish, that if the person with the disability doesn't learn they themselves will look incompetent and people will think badly of them.

Additionally some staff may realise that quite a deal of their self-respect comes from the fact that they are good at their staff role. They may feel uncomfortable, depressed and perhaps threatened if they believe that their specific expertise (on which they pride themselves) may not be appropriate when it comes to teaching, managing or leading a person with a disability. (Their specific expertise may in fact be just right, but they may not recognise that, yet).

Staff may feel confused.   Staff may hear conflicting information from the many available sources of advice: the previous community, the current doctor, the parents of the person, friends who know a person 'just like that' or other staff of people with similar diagnoses.

Not only is advice confusing, but sometimes it is hard to find specific advice. The available literature on the diagnosis may not mention the particular concern, and other staff, experienced with people who have similar disabilities, may not have noticed the specific concern, either.

Subtle confusion can arise from the message 'You're a skilled staff member, you're capable' which is at odds with the unspoken message 'You need help'. 'This person with a disability doesn't need special staff' is at odds with the hordes of hovering specialists and the 'special' books and in-service courses that staff are offered!

Confusion, however, can be the beginning of the realisation that not all good advice is 'out there' but that most good advice is common sense available right here.

Staff may feel pressured and tired.   Anything unfamiliar, any constant source of uncertainty, is tiring. Staff may feel pressure from other people to be prepared, to plan for meetings and to provide documentation; they may feel that they are not given enough time for the extra roles and tasks which integration has brought them. They may add pressure to themselves by setting a standard of always looking positive, never looking hassled, always being one step ahead and never bothering other people with requests for help.

Staff may feel excited. There are also staff members who not only recognise the social justice of integration and its positive outcomes, but who want to take some responsibility for making it happen. In addition, some staff are thankful for the opportunity to do so. They may simply accept integration as an opportunity for personal challenge and for new skill development. They may approach integration as they approached other challenges in their professional life—multi-grade classes, computerised accounts, new piecework rates, overnight adventure camps—as one of the delights their job offers them.

It's a challenge! I chose teaching as a challenge. That's what I'm here for.

Staff may feel proud. Staff may feel proud that their boss has felt they are capable of making integration work, or that a person with a disability or his parents have chosen their community. They may be excited and stimulated by the prospect of new paths to cross and skills to gain. They may feel rewarded by any skills the person gains, by their own growth and by the growth of the other people in their community. They may feel proud and satisfied at having met a challenge creatively.

Sure, they may also feel afraid, unfamiliar, uncertain, uncomfortable at times, confused and quite often tired, but they are loving every moment of it!

THE COMMUNITY'S PERSPECTIVE

Many activities have a sub-community of their own whose involvement is vital to the ongoing spirit of the activity; sporting groups, clubs and certainly schools are examples of this. Parent and volunteer support and involvement at these activities greatly influences the atmosphere and attitudes of the group, including the group's attitude towards integration.

There is also a community of everyday life—individuals who may not know each other as a group and who are busy going about their everyday lives. They occasionally meet a person who has a disability—down the street, on the train, in a line. Thus, many people are part of the community of the person with the disability; they are involved with integration irrespective of their opinions and of their desire for involvement. Even by ignoring the situation they are reacting. They may not consider this reaction their 'opinion about integration', but their reaction is part of their feelings about people with a disability being in such places.

Additionally, people who have a disability often have a community that revolves round their disability: a doctor/therapist/treatment community. They may also be involved in a wider community related to their particular disability: the 'blind' community, the 'deaf' community, 'retarded people'.

Many of these communities have feelings about integration—a group opinion about the role of integration: a scout group may encourage children with a disability to join and 'do their best'; a therapist may feel that children with cerebral palsy learn best at a special school unless they can manage their own wheelchair; the 'blind' community may feel that children who are blind more easily learn braille at a school for blind children than at a regular school.

Individual community members may also have an opinion about integration and it may vary from their community's opinion. Whether as part of a group or as an individual, people's opinions of integration will be as diverse as the individuals who make up the community.

People may not care.

> Some people believe that discussion about people with a disability in the community or out of it, in regular schools or special schools, in the house next door or the hostel up the road is someone else's responsibility. They leave the debate and decisions about such topics to other people; they are disinterested.[5]

They get on with whatever happens, just as they have paid their taxes and coped with inflation without complaining, and read about men on the moon and Fax machines without understanding them. These people may have no personal opinion about integration but follow community consensus.

People may want nothing to do with integration.
Some community members want nothing to do with integration. Like some staff members, they believe that people with a disability are best put away and forgotten. They may make a donation to 'those poor spastic souls', 'the wee blind babies', 'the retards, God love them' or the 'victims of epilepsy', and then feel that the needs of such people with a disability will be met.

Other community members may acknowledge people with a disability but feel negative about integration.

> Disabled people are too intrusive. There are already too many people with disabilities in the community having an adverse effect on crime statistics.[6]

These community members believe that integration won't work and don't really want to discuss the possibility of it working, even though their reasons for these negative feelings may be unclear.

People may want to know more.
Some community members feel interested in integration but feel impartial. Their impartiality may change (either negatively or positively) as they experience integration, but it may also be influenced by strong opinions (either negative or positive) held by other members of their community. These people are prepared to act—to give integration a go or to raise objections to it—depending on the opinion of their community. Although prepared to give integration a go, they may not know what to do or say to help make integration work.

People may totally support integration. Some community members feel that integration is a positive force and reflects a natural sense of order. They may believe they have a role to play and want to take responsibility for their part in making integration happen.

COMMUNITY FEELINGS ABOUT INTEGRATION

Community members' feelings, just like those of parents and staff, may change over time and may vary according to the person whom they are considering.

> Oh, Bill. He's not disabled. He just lost his leg in the war and he's okay. I'm talking about those spastic ones.

People may feel unfamiliar and uncertain. Community members currently see people with a disability more frequently than in previous decades. They often see them in 'new' situations such as regular schools, shops, work or parties, rather than in 'old' situations like on a group outing or collecting money for a charitable group. Unfamiliarity with such situations can make people curious and their curiosity may seem unnatural or exaggerated. This unfamiliarity may leave them feeling uncertain of the right thing to say or do, so they may do nothing.

People may feel confused. Some people are bound by old views of disability and feel confused when they see people with a disability participating in activities they had thought were meaningless or not 'allowed': going to work, living on their own, driving a car, blind people going to the movies or retarded children going to regular school. Their knowledge about people with a disability may be outdated, and they may act inappropriately.

> Did you hear the story about the woman in the wheelchair who had bought a can of soft drink and was holding it between her legs and someone came up and put 10c in it. . . . The story is not fictitious. The 10c coin ruined the drink.[7]

People may feel afraid. People often think in stereotyped ways about people with particular disabilities: 'Spastic people fall over', 'Epileptics need constant supervision' or 'Mental people can't remember things and get lost'. People with such stereotyped views feel afraid of what might happen and of their ability to deal with their feelings when they meet a person with a disability, so they avoid such people.

People may feel worried about their own interests. Some people are concerned that integration will cause a disadvantage to themselves and to other people who don't have a disability. Parents of children who attend activities with children who have a disability may worry that their child will 'miss out' in some way or suffer as a result of integration: perhaps pick up bad language or bad habits or that standards will drop. Some parents of children without a disability worry that if their child likes and plays with a

The perils of categorisation

child who *has* a disability that their non-disabled child will be seen as 'odd' and not able to make 'normal' friends.

People may not doubt the value of integration for the person with the disability but they may want reassurance that other people are not going to miss out or be disadvantaged.

> I worry that my child gets less of the teacher's time now that Jane is in her class.

> I don't know why they go to the football. Those spastics don't watch it anyway and they get the best seats down the front, too.

> John's got a disability, I know, but he's getting all that government money to redo his bathroom. Why should he get that money? My bathroom needs a bit of work too.

THE COMMUNITY LEADERS' PERSPECTIVE

Community leaders—school principals, group leaders, employers, bosses and people with higher responsibilities—may have a different perspective of integration to that of other staff who are in more direct contact with a person who has a disability. Leaders have responsibilities not just for this year and this person but also for next year, for other people with a disability and for all the other community members of their school, club or workplace.

Just as direct contact staff often have mixed feelings about integration, so may community leaders. They may have concerns about philosophical issues (perhaps their personal philosophy is different to their organisation's), about administrative and policy issues (resources and consensus), about legal and union issues and about the rights, fears and needs of other community members (other staff, community members, parents and volunteers).

Knowledge about people's different perspectives promotes a broader and more rational understanding of the issues that surround integration and of why it is sometimes rough going. It identifies areas where views diverge and where acknowledgement of these diverse viewpoints must be made for integration to work.

PART TWO: **SET?**

Part two sets the scene for the integration of an individual person with particular abilities and difficulties into a specific community.

If a person has severe or multiple disabilities or is not used to regular communities, the ideas about choosing a community and preparation may need careful consideration, and the community may want to carefully develop a plan for integration. In other circumstances people may decide to directly use only parts of this information, particularly if the person with whom they are concerned has minimal disabilities, is already familiar with the community and the community is already familiar with him.

No matter people's past involvement with integration, new situations are an opportunity to establish a firm footing that leads to the best sort of integration for everyone—real chances and real choices.

Part two outlines factors to help establish each 'new' integration situation in a way that leaves everyone informed, prepared and set to give it a go.

Chapter Five

CHOOSING A COMMUNITY

Some parents of children with a disability feel that 'choosing a community' into which they will integrate their child is an odd sort of idea. There is no choice in their mind, because for them integration means that their child will do everything that their family does, go everywhere that their family goes and join the same activities that their other children join.

Many people with a disability are already involved with community activities and 'starting integration' may never have been a specific thought. Likewise, the staff at many community activities are already involved with people who have a disability. However, no matter people's past involvement with integration, new situations or changes in situation (a new babysitter or childcare centre, a change of neighbourhood or job, starting basketball or self-defence, joining a bus tour or having work experience) are opportunities to establish integration on a firm footing.

Parents may integrate their child into some regular community activities without making a conscious choice, perhaps into the local playgroup or Sunday school. However when considering other sorts of activities these same parents may spend time looking for the 'best' community. Such careful considerations are often for more lasting situations like school or employment, where parents feel that choosing the right community will be important for their child's long-term, genuine acceptance and involvement—for real integration. Frequently these sort of communities are those that, in the past, have not commonly been attended by people who have a disability.

For many parents, caregivers and service providers there are times when choosing the right community becomes an issue, sometimes a big issue: attend a large school or a small rural school; build the residential unit in this suburb or that; choose this employment situation or the other.

'Choosing a community' should not be an issue—a person with a disability should have the same chances and choices as other people and be able to be involved in any aspect of community life she wishes. It should not be a matter of 'integrating' her but should, instead, be a matter of her joining a community because that is the one she wants to join, just as other people choose and join communities. Maybe she prefers one swimming club to another because she likes their club colours, or chooses one elderly citizens club instead of another because her friends already go there. The choice has nothing to do with her disability.

Having less than an ideal environment at times is part of everyone's life. It could be suggested that by choosing the 'best' environment a person with a disability is being denied the good and the bad, the give and take of life. This is true to some extent, but for many people who have a disability all their environments are far from ideal, so any choice is really only making the best of more limited and less suitable choices anyway. The choices available to a person with a disability are usually not as varied as those of people without a disability: to see the film in Cinema 1 or Cinema 2? (whereas the movie the person really wants to see is on at Cinema 3 which has no wheelchair access); children's aerobics or gym? (whereas the person really wants to learn ballet but they have a limp).

Through life people try to reduce the difficulties they have, to make circumstances more favourable and to have more of the good things. Weighing up the good and bad aspects of available choices is thus not at odds with normalisation (chapter 2) but is a normal part of life for most people: a good, but distant job or a less appealing job closer to home? A big house with a lot of housework or a small house that seems poky? People choose a community which best meets the specific purpose they have in mind (to learn, to live in peace, to work or to relax) and where they are wanted and respected. This is human nature.

Parents often weigh up the various aspects of choices they have for any of their children: learn-to-swim lessons or a competitive swimming coach; an emphasis on sport or music or academic subjects at school; individual skill development or team spirit at football? Similarly, people who have a disability or the parents of a child with a disability may do this weighing up in relation to choosing a school, club, job or house. It may be little different to the weighing up that other people do, though there may be additional information that they require in order to help them choose the 'right' community.

People weigh up the various aspects of a community according to their own priorities: one person favours the good job despite the travel distance, another the short travel distance despite the less appealing job; one person favours a large house and garden despite the housework, another the increased leisure time that a small easy-maintenance house and garden can provide. Likewise the priorities of people involved with integration differ: one parent of a child with a disability favours the local school irrespective of its attitudes or facilities, another a more distant school with the 'right' environment; one parent favours the same scout pack as his other children attend, another a different scout pack. For reasons that are important to themselves but may be unimportant to other people, they make different decisions.

People who have a disability are being integrated more often and into a wider variety of community activities than previously: not just going to the synagogue but taking the Bar Mitzvah, not just going to primary school but going on to secondary school and tertiary education, not just employed to wipe tables at the fast food shop but (surprise!) to serve customers, not just going on a day trip to the beach but (shock! horror!) travelling overseas. This experience—greater numbers of people with a disability doing more activities more often in ordinary communities—provides information which can be used to help other people with a disability be just as successful in taking up the chances and choices they have.

THE 'BEST' COMMUNITY

'A community is a group of people who come together for a common purpose and who are needed to maintain that purpose. A school is a community and so is a neighbourhood, club, shopping centre, workplace or childcare centre. A community includes all its participants, no matter their role: bosses, staff, volunteers, people participating in the community's activities and their families' (chapter 1). Each community is unique because it combines the individuality of all its members, no matter their role; each member is unique, including those who have a disability.

There are many factors to consider in defining the 'best' community: environments, attitudes, programs, facilities and people. Additionally, the 'best' community is only best for one person. 'The best brownie pack in the district', 'The right suburb for everyone' and 'The best school for integration' simply do not exist as people want and value different aspects of a situation, and are prepared to make different compromises.

However careful consideration of any choice will help make it a better choice for the person doing the choosing. This is just as true of 'choosing a new dress' as it is of 'choosing a community'. Consideration may be given to the individual needs and wants of the person with the disability and her family, and to the ability of any particular community under consideration to meet those needs. Additionally consideration may be given to general community characteristics which are more likely to make integration work.

INDIVIDUAL CONSIDERATIONS

What is the overall goal of integration for this person? Keeping an overall goal in mind helps in defining the type of community needed. When a person with a disability joins a community his goals may not be the same or have the same priority as those of other community members. A boy who has a disability may join scouts for the same reasons as other boys (to learn some skills and develop a sense of belonging) or for different reasons (to experience the behaviour, interests and language of other young boys). A teenage girl in a wheelchair may join a youth club for the same reasons as other teenagers (to make friends, participate in social outings and go on camps) or for the particular reason of meeting teenagers who don't have a disability. She may also join to consciously participate in the club's social service efforts, as she may often have been on the 'receiving' end of assistance, but never on the 'giving' end. The particular scout pack or youth club chosen may vary, depending on the overall goal.

What are this person's needs? Knowledge about the general needs and wants of the person who has the disability is important in choosing a community. Once she has joined, her needs and wants can be more clearly defined and specifically matched to the community's programs. An individual planning committee (chapter 8) may do this by fine-tuning overall goals, by identifying priorities and specific objectives, and by developing a program. However a general understanding of the person's needs will help a community be chosen which has the potential to appropriately do this fine-tuning and development.

What community does this person want to join?   Integration is about choices, and the person who has the disability may have particular preferences about the type of community he wants to join, and even about which particular one.

> *A parent*:   John always wanted to go on a camp.

> *A parent*:   John wants to go to school with Simon and Sally and wear the same uniform as them. He doesn't want some other school.

Is a special unit within a regular community appropriate?   Some people believe that integration only happens in ordinary communities, that integration is not real if it is happening somewhere else, somewhere 'special'. They think that special anything—special schools, special houses, special programs—reduces people's chances and choices.

Other people believe that *special units* within a regular community offer good opportunities for some people: perhaps a deaf unit within a regular school, a special group at a swimming club or a special parking place at a supermarket. However, sometimes it is the 'special services' in the special unit that are wanted, not the special unit in total. The special services may not be available in the regular community in which the unit is placed, but only in the special unit.

For a special unit to offer the best chances and choices, a person's time and activities there should always be matched to specific goals (chapter 8), and there should be appropriate opportunities for him to spend time in the regular community in which the unit is placed. Integration is not just being on the same site together but involves interacting, taking risks and responsibilities.

For special units to be successful, the staff of the units must be part of the staff of the whole community. Staff members need to have status and the unit needs to have some organisational power within the whole community. Unless this happens, 'special unit' may just imply 'special staff' for 'special people', a situation where differences are stressed; this does not help integration work.

Is reverse integration appropriate?   Some communities establish *reverse integration* where people without a disability attend a community that is primarily for people who have a disability: regular scouts attending a 'special scouts' group, regular students attending a 'school for blind children'. For people who have spent a long time in segregated communities

Segregation limits experiences and learning

this may be a good way to begin integration. It may also be an appropriate long-term form of integration for some people, particularly if they need complicated large pieces of equipment like computer communication devices or respirators. (But don't think that these pieces of equipment can't be moved out just because it has not been done before; the individual planning committee [chapter 8] may think of a way!)

It is also important that short periods of reverse integration don't become just a reverse 'social visit' (chapter 8) unless this is an identified part of a larger integration plan.

Is it best to use the same community as other family members?

The issue of 'a child who has a disability attending a different community to the one his brothers and sisters attend', is frequently considered for some types of activities, (long-term activities like school) but rarely for other types of activities (like church). There is no 'right' answer.

> *A parent*: I have all my children at the one school because when they bring their friends home they already know about John and it is no big deal.

> *A parent*: I have Jane at a different school to my other two children. I think they need time away from her to develop their own friendships.

If the children from one family do all go to the same community, many parents advise clearly establishing rules.

I told the staff that I didn't want Sally to be given any more responsibility for Jane than other older sisters.

Is it appropriate to travel to a 'better' community? Travel may initially seem a small issue, but it is worth careful consideration because choosing a more distant community which seems 'better' may defeat the purpose of integration. Travel can become not only an inconvenience and a source of distress for some people, but also a social barrier. A person who lives in one neighbourhood but joins a community in another may be seen as 'different' and thus integration will be hampered. Distance can make it more difficult to participate in the social environment of the community: after-school play networks, transport rosters and casual social contacts. These are all things that can help a person belong to a community.

Know your own thresholds. People can consider their thresholds (chapter 12) for particular community characteristics in order to help establish their priorities and clarify the limits of the community that will be 'best' for them. How much involvement do the parents want with the community? Are they prepared to give as much as, or more than is expected of other parents? Some parents are prepared to give a lot to the community in all sorts of ways but there may be a limit in terms of amount (number of days on canteen duty) or in terms of kind (canteen duty but not excursion duty). Parents sometimes prefer not to have a closer involvement in the community with their own child than is usual for other parents; they will help but in ways that don't directly involve their child.

COMMUNITY CHARACTERISTICS ABOUT WHICH TO FEEL HOPEFUL

No single community has only 'good' signs. In evaluating communities, a person is really looking for one where the 'not-so-good' signs are not high on their list of priorities. They are looking for the most appropriate community for their situation but which has the *potential to become even more appropriate*.

A well organised community is ready for integration. Organised communities are more likely to let integration start and to keep it going. They can support integration because they:

- Communicate well and their members know what is going on.
- Clearly let members understand their role in the group.
- Have a decision-making process that members understand, know how to participate in and abide by.
- Have a problem-solving attitude to events that happen; they don't just hope problems will go away but do something about them, often finding creative solutions.

- Share responsibility and put trust in their members to carry out this responsibility.
- Have an overall plan. They usually plan ahead and don't make last minute changes without informing people.

An energetic community can keep integration going. Integration may take extra planning and preparation by the community (chapters 6 and 7). Communities that have shown they are ready for this:

- Like hearing about new ideas.
- Share ideas and don't keep information to themselves.
- Don't shirk hard physical work or detailed organisation.
- Are among the first of their kind to try new ideas: a school trying cross-age tutoring, a club trying new fundraising ideas.
- Don't look for outside help immediately a problem arises but look instead to re-organise the resources, skills and talents they already have within their community.
- Volunteer rather than wait to be asked (or rather than hope they won't be asked).
- Continue to improve the quality of what they can offer members.

Leaders and staff set an example. A community is only as good as its leader, be it the boss at work, the principal at school or the scout leader. The leader usually reflects the feelings of the group; she has been elected because she represents their beliefs. Communities that are open to integration select leaders who are open to integration, leaders who:

- Are positive, confident and enjoy their work.
- Like people.
- Understand the organisation of their community and stick to its policies, purpose and future directions.
- Support whatever decisions the community makes, even if contrary to their personal beliefs.
- Are patient and persistent and understand the value of hard work without always expecting quick results.
- Are aware that their attitudes affect the attitudes of members and staff, and are prepared to set an example.
- Are confident enough to be individual in their way of working while still reflecting the values of the group.
- Are open to new ideas and work well with other people; they recognise other people's expertise and value their input.

The development of policies indicates organisation. A community that has policies about any aspect of its function (behaviour, dress codes, discipline or financial matters) is sufficiently organised to see that integration can happen. Good policies indicate that the community:

- Plans ahead.
- Sees the needs of the total group as well as of individual members.
- Tries to provide rights for its members and to protect those rights.
- Has an individual identity rather than having a policy copied from a similar group.
- Doesn't see members as a problem, but instead sees a problem as a lack of proper planning for that member.
- Sees integration as one of many important issues and doesn't let integration override other issues.
- Sees integration as a process that is happening now with this person but will also happen in the future.

A rational approach to resources and facilities indicates a positive perspective.   A community which realises that integration relies more on attitudes and interaction than on attendance alone keeps the issue of facilities and resources in perspective. A community indicates that it understands integration when its first step is to re-organise its existing resources (rather than demand 'extra' or 'special' resources) and when it uses them in the least disruptive way.

A focus on tasks indicates action.   A community that focuses on what needs to be done and how to get it done rather than on people's personalities or on problems, is one that helps integration become a reality. By focusing on a task, a community shows:

- An understanding of the process that is happening rather than getting caught up in one particular example. It focuses on its ability to 'provide a program for children with a wide range of abilites' rather than on its ability to 'provide a program for John'.
- A willingness to use the system to meet the needs of individuals within it rather than working on individuals to fit into the system. The community uses the system to 'help John' rather than try to make John 'more normal' or 'easier' to fit into the existing system.
- It can see the whole task and also the small steps needed to complete the task; it can see the whole community and also individual members.

Attitudes are important.   A community's attitudes to any minority or less powerful group gives an indication of its attitude to the integration of a person with a disability into its membership. No particular attitude can be taken in isolation as an indicator of good things or bad things. At the prospect of integrating a person with a disability, a staff attitude of unquenchable enthusiasm may be good, but so may considered caution.

> *A parent*:   Mr Leader carefully thought about it as he said he would, and got back to us when he said he would. I thought it showed he was thorough and not rash, which was good.

Chances: everyone can be a star

A parent: Miss Staff loved the idea of a challenge. When I mentioned Jane joining the club next year, she immediately wanted to know when Jane could start, no questions asked, and I was thrilled.

The principles of integration (chapter 1) can be supported by both individual and staff attitudes like:

- Working for the good of the group, not just for personal benefit.
- Taking some responsibility for the total community not just for their part of the community.
- Understanding and tolerating differences—different ages, sexes and abilities.
- Respecting differences: valuing the wise contributions of the elderly and the enthusiasm of the young, non-judgementally learning about international customs.
- Stressing abilities not differences; valuing a person's skills no matter what they are.

A parent: My child has lax joints and can do the splits incredibly well. When the other kids are showing off—shooting goals, doing handstands—they sometimes ask him to do the splits because they know he is good at it, not because it is odd. It's kind of nice.

- Considering people as individuals, showing an attitude of reality and practicality, not of an academic discussion.

A parent: After I went and saw them at the school they asked if they could come and see John at preschool. I knew then that they weren't seeing him just like the other spastic children they had at the school.

- A preparedness to admit mistakes.

A parent: Mr Leader panicked, but the fourth person he rang he listened to at great length and it obviously made a lot of sense to him. He knew he'd been a bit silly and now we even laugh about how panicky he was.

COMMUNITY CHARACTERISTICS ABOUT WHICH TO FEEL WARY

Although no situation will be all 'bad', there are some signs which indicate that integration may be difficult to get going and difficult to keep working.

Rigid communities deny individuality. Some communities stick by the rules at all cost even when it is obvious that common sense is needed. Rigid groups say 'These are the rules; there is nothing I can do about it', rather than seeing rules as a framework to be continually reviewed. They may even use the rules to do nothing.

A parent: I asked the club about Jane joining aerobics. They said they'd not been asked before and that they'd have to ask the manager. He was overseas. They'd let me know. He was always still overseas when I rang.

Communities that stress minimum standards, that hide differences, that focus on deficits or 'catching up' will have difficulty understanding and fostering the growth of individual members.

Communities that panic lack perspective. If staff become immobile with panic at the suggestion of integration, then they probably don't have a process that will keep integration going. Initial concern can be a prompt for useful action but continued panic indicates a lack of process and organisation. Such communities call many directionless meetings, seek many outside opinions, involve numerous people and are unable to settle down to the real issues and the real individual. They often seek maximum available resources at the mention of the words 'disability' or 'integration' before they have met the individual or know her needs.

A school administrator: The teacher rang to ask for an assistant in the group and after five minutes conversation I found out he'd never seen or met the child but knew one 'just like her'.

A parent: The guidance officer had rung the school to make a date to discuss my son's integration. All the staff immediately joined the union and called a meeting to put a freeze on accepting him until resources were available. They hadn't met him; they didn't even know if he needed resources.

Communities that dislike new ideas lack energy. A community that says 'No, that wouldn't work', 'We tried that once and so and so happened', 'But who'd do the work?' to any new idea is probably not ready and able to give integration the attention and energy it deserves. These communities like things as they are: 'We've never done that before', 'I don't think our members would like that'. For them integration may be an even bigger step than other simpler new ideas they've had trouble implementing.

Labels can deny individuality. Even simple and commonly used labels —'kiddies', 'girlies', 'our slow group' or 'Mums and Dads'—can make it more difficult to see the individual behind the label. People that use such labels may find it difficult to cater for the individual behind the label of 'disability'. It can be difficult to entirely avoid using labels, but the least judgemental labels are best: 'our grade 4 students', 'girls', 'our younger group' or 'Mr and Mrs Evans, Mr and Mrs Butler'.

> *A parent*: Mr Leader said: 'We've already got one of those here', and I knew that he thought Jane was going to be the same as another Down syndrome child they had at the school and he thought Jane would need exactly the same help.

Communities can use integration to provide status. Some communities are proud of the fact they are flexible and creative enough to provide real participation and interaction for a person with a disability. They may be just as proud of their other achievements: a record cake-stall income, largest attendance or winning the interclub competition.

However some communities seek glory for having integrated a person with a disability; they are just reverting back to the charitable, 'do-gooder' values that stop real integration working. Integration may be a token gesture they are making in order to further their own needs.

ACTION FOR PARENTS

(This section is primarily for parents of people with a disability who are considering and comparing communities.)

Get organised. Make a checklist of organisations that can help and read any literature that they have available. Make a checklist of people that can help and talk to them. Prepare a list of questions you want answered before making a decision, perhaps basing this on 'individual considerations'. Prepare a list of possible communities.

Get some help. An advocate (chapter 9) can help parents in many ways: finding information, visiting, asking questions, assessing the answers. They can help plan the person's attendance when a community has been chosen by becoming part of the individual planning committee (chapter 8).

Professionals may be able to assist in considering communities and even offer advice, but make sure that they know the particular person and the specific community. Professionals can also be a link between parents of people with a disability at similar communities.

Self-help groups (chapter 9) may offer literature and advice, and perhaps contacts with other parents in similar situations or those who have current involvement with particular communities.

Visit a few communities.   Don't just visit the community you've heard about; visit a few communities and make good use of the visits. Don't just visit on open day but on ordinary days, too. Ask to see the community's policies on various issues including integration. Note any situations or conversations which clash with individual considerations or which indicate a 'characteristic about which to be wary' or a 'characteristic about which to feel hopeful'.

Does this community have a co-ordinating person responsible for community members who have a disability—an integration teacher, a special needs recreation officer?

Talk to the community leader. Some parents interview him as though he is an applicant for the job of managing their child and the accompanying resource package.

Talk to other people in a similar situation.   Talking to other parents involved with integration may help parents clarify their own thoughts and priorities. They can visit communities together, ask different questions and perhaps get a broader picture than if they had visited alone; their opinions may differ, but talking may help clarify their concerns.

Talk to other people who attend the communities under consideration.   Talk to other people in the community—staff, community members or parents of members. Their attitudes (to each other, to differences, to parents, to people who have a disability) can be a good indicator of how they will accept and involve a person with a disability.

Try a few communities.   Many communities have orientation sessions for potential participants, perhaps a *trial period* before joining (chapter 7).

Some communities have 'taster' or 'have-a-go' programs for potential participants to try before committing themselves. Other communities offer members experience in a variety of programs (or sub-communities) before they need make a decision about joining any particular one. These are excellent examples of real choice based on real experience.

Remember the self-talk phrase (chapter 16) 'Nothing is forever'. Choosing a community is like any other decision—it is only a decision that seems best for 'now'. Circumstances, programs or people may change and another community may become the 'best' at some other time.

As more communities understand integration, allow it to happen and see it as their responsibility, 'choosing a community' will cease to be a chore. It will merely be a matter of choosing a community where friends go, where the service is good, where the team is a winner or where a person can feel at home—ordinary reasons for joining an ordinary community.

Chapter Six

ATTENDANCE AT A COMMUNITY: PLANS AND POLICIES

'While acknowledging the differences between communities, integration aims to ensure that within each community all members have the same chances and choices' (chapter 1). Effective planning helps provide more chances and choices for all community members.

Sometimes planning is done automatically and casually:

- 'I wonder if the Forum cinema is wheelchair accessible? I'd better ring.'
- 'I'd better take some straws for Jane to use in case Helen doesn't have any.'
- 'Does the picnic area have a fence? I'd better take John's football; he doesn't wander so much when he has that to play with.'

Sometimes planning is more formal than this and is done well in advance, involving various people, discussions and decisions.

- 'We want all sorts of people to be able to use this community room we're planning. We'll need to consider lighting, acoustics, access for prams and wheelchairs, and safety for young children.'

An effective integration plan can be part of a community's overall plan to be a well-organised, energetic community that flexibly responds to the needs of the group and of individual members. Planning is the ingredient quoted again and again when people are asked about successful integration: 'good planning', 'early planning', 'detailed planning', 'a collaborative plan', 'an overall plan and specific goals'.

A good integration plan blends all the skills that different people have to offer—experience, enthusiasm, specialised skills and individuality; it also recognises, understands and allows for people's positive and not-so-positive feelings. Planning can become uncomfortable when it involves many people, new surroundings, discussions about fears and hopes, political and personal viewpoints, arguments about money, descriptions of similarities and differences or rhetoric about needs and rights. (Sometimes everything seems to be discussed except the person who has the disability!) A good plan can help reduce these feelings and provide a sense of common purpose.

Planning for integration is important because it sets the scene for a long time to come. It indicates how seriously a community feels about integra-

Social justice: planning considers all community members

tion, how much time and effort it is prepared to allocate and how realistic it is. It can affect not just the integration of this person today, but the integration of many people next month and next year.

An effective integration plan involves both considerations about the community (to provide for people who have a disability) and considerations about particular people who have a disability (to match their needs to the community's programs and facilities). The plans for each particular person (individual integration programs) are discussed fully in chapter 8, while this chapter discusses the community's plan for people with a disability—its general plans and policies, and those that relate specifically to integration.

A COMMUNITY'S POLICIES

All of a community's policies reflect its attitudes. Each of a community's written or unwritten laws, policies, guidelines or principles should be based on the principle of social justice—all people have equal value. Irrespective of whether a community has a specific integration policy, each of its policies can reflect attitudes that understand the needs of all community members including those who have a disability.

Overall community goals reflect social justice. A community's overall goals take account of the needs of all its members including those who have a disability or are disadvantaged: children and adults, males and females, people who are blind or in wheelchairs, people who are fat, pregnant, active or lazy, people with various ethnic, religious and political backgrounds.

Community members are not categorised. People are individuals. Any services or treatment that community members receive, or any contributions that they make to a community should be based on their individual abilities, not on categorisation by age, sex, nationality, disability, income or any other attribute.

Community members are not segregated. If people aren't categorised, they are less likely to be separated out and kept aside from the community. They are more likely to be given equal opportunities to participate, to belong and to become accepted into a community, to be integrated into a community.

Community members have equal opportunities. All people have the right to be treated equally. No person should be discriminated against or treated less favourably than another; neither should rules and conditions exist in the community that make it more difficult for some people to be able to participate than for others.

Community members have choices. People need a variety of experiences. Real choices can only be made when a person is offered a whole range of experiences from which to choose. Society will change its perception of people who have a disability when such people themselves choose the services they want and when those services are accountable, like any other service, to the consumer (the person with the disability).

Community members are allowed to take risks. People learn and grow through taking risks. Equal opportunity means not only making choices, but also taking responsibility for those choices—being allowed to make a risky choice while knowing the risks, acknowledging responsibility for the choice and being dignified in the subsequent success or failure.

The least restrictive environment is available. (This can also be called the least restrictive alternative). If the freedom and dignity of individuals is important, then there is a need to limit the control which people or services can impose on other people. Provision of the least restrictive environment means that decisions which affect other people should not intrude unnecessarily in their lives. The least restrictive environment presumes that there is a wide range of services available, and it provides a way of ordering and evaluating these options to maximise the chances of real integration happening. From among the available situations, the least restrictive alternative is usually the least segregating one, the one that offers ordinary peer models, functional learning, chances, choices and variety (chapter 2). Large institutions are usually more restrictive than small institutions, small institutions more restrictive than community residential units, swimming lessons exclusively for boys with a disability more restrictive than regular community swimming lessons for children of both sexes.

A COMMUNITY INTEGRATION COMMITTEE

Some communities establish a formal 'integration committee' to develop their general integration plan. The committee is composed of various people within the community, often including 'decision-makers', staff and community representatives; it may also include people from other communities.

When making its plan, the community integration committee doesn't have in mind particular people or particular disabilities; the committee is not developing a program for an individual person but instead a general plan to allow any person with any disability to join the community.

AN INTEGRATION POLICY

Some communities develop their general integration plan into an 'integration policy' and this is usually done by the integration committee. (In this book, the terms 'community integration plan' and 'integration policy' are interchangeable.) Such a policy outlines the community's belief in integration and contains an overview of integration as it applies to their community. It usually lists the community's existing resources: programs, staff, equipment and any community networks. An integration policy should also help community members recognise what they can do to facilitate integration; it should let all the members of the community learn more about integration and about their part in making it work.

However, legislating for the rights of a particular group of people may only harden existing prejudices and create negative attitudes. To avoid this, an integration policy needs to be seen as a specific example of the community's wider policies. It is not 'favouritism for people with a disability' but an example of how social justice can be applied to particular community members.

Integration doesn't aim to change the purpose, rules or regulations of communities or to make them all alike. So the principles of integration will be used in different ways by different communities. (Similarly an architect can design a number of ideal homes that all comply with the laws of physics and the principles of an ideal home.)

An integration policy developed by one community will not entirely suit another similar community (a different school or another club) because each community's facilities and resources are unique. However one community's integration policy may provide good ideas that can be used to develop a suitable integration policy for another community.

Integration policies vary in format and in the issues they address: 'enrolment', 'program', 'resources', 'preparation' or 'review'. Despite differences in format or content, a good integration policy provides a formal structure that makes integration possible. This formal structure then supports the social processes that make integration most likely to happen.

Although an integration policy alone will not make integration happen, the principle of social justice underlying it can be used to help integration happen. (Similarly an ideal home may never have been built before but an architect can use the laws of physics and the principles of an ideal home to attempt to design one.) A good integration policy reflects not only the social justice that underlies all of the community's policies, but also additional factors that relate to the specific social justice issue of integration:

Overall community goals for integration are needed. Goals in an integration policy identify ways to reduce the handicapping effect of disabilities, and of increasing community members' participation in programs. Such goals may include making facilities safer, easier and more suitable for all members; broadening the community's programs and thus their appeal, and helping people be more tolerant of individual differences.

Integration is ongoing. A good integration policy recognises that integration is an issue of social justice, not a fad; integration is ongoing. The community doesn't make an 'exception' this year based on one leader's kindness or on a person-to-person deal (perhaps between a parent and a staff member), but instead sets a precedent that ensures opportunities for people with a disability now and in the future.

Integration means participation and interdependence. Integration doesn't mean just attendance. It means active sustained participation in community activities; it means interaction and interdependence among community members. A good integration policy doesn't allow for a person with a disability to become an island (or part of an island) that happens to be in the mainstream. The policy helps the person to become part of the mainstream. The policy encourages and provides for attendance of people with a disability, and develops processes to support their participation in community programs.

Plans to reach the overall goals are needed. The community needs not only overall goals for community members but also plans to reach those goals. Such plans may mean legislative changes or the provision of money for equipment, personnel and programs. It may mean the development of new activities or the modification of existing ones. It may mean instituting organisational changes within the community, like changing staff responsibilities or rosters.

The community's existing resources are used.   Of course integration uses the community's resources—that is what integration is about. A good integration policy makes sure that a person with a disability knows of and can use the various programs and resources that the community has, by outlining:

- *Current programs* and their flexibility in attendance times and locations. Are library services available to home-bound people as well as being centre-based? Can students study externally as well as on campus? Are shorter session times possible?

- *The community's physical facilities.* Are the facilites at the various program locations suitable for program participants? (Checklists of environmental considerations for people from specific disability groups are available from resource services [chapter 10].)

- *Personnel* within the community who can assist with integration. These people may be staff members who have experience with people who have a disability, experience with integration, or who have responsibility to assist with integration; they may be volunteers or other community members who have a disability and can offer advice from their own experience.

- *Equipment* which is available. An integration policy may include an appendix of equipment within the community which can assist with integration (hoists, ramps, large print materials), including the equipment's availability, portability and booking procedures.

- *Connections with other communities* that can help make integration work. Some communities are part of established networks that share ideas and resources and can help integration be more successful in each of the communities.

Additional resources may be required.   Individual planning committees (chapter 8) may request additional resources in order to support the integration of the particular person with whom they are concerned. The integration policy outlines the process that the community will use to respond to such requests. How will the community distribute the resources it currently has available? What access does the community have to additional resources and how can individual planning committees request these?

Staff and community preparation for and education about integration may be needed.   A good integration policy recognises that attitudes play an important part in the success of integration (chapter 3) and it plans for appropriate preparation and ongoing education.

Each person with a disability requires an individual integration program.   The community's integration policy establishes the community's general support for integration but recognises the need for additional specific planning for each person with a disability—they each need an individual integration program matching their needs to the community's programs (chapter 8). This matching will best be done by individual planning committees (chapter 8) composed of people who know the person with the disability. It will not be done by the community's integration committee who may only know about the community or about disability generally, not about the person specifically.

A good integration policy recognises, plans for and perhaps co-ordinates many individual planning committees.

A community's plan for integration must be reviewed. A regular review is a positive response to the active process of integration, more positive than an ad-hoc change which is only a knee-jerk reaction to problems that arise. Regularly scheduled reviews allow continual monitoring and altering of the integration process as needs change, as more information is gathered and as alternative resources become available.

An integration policy which includes overall goals allows an evaluation of whether those goals have been reached. A regular review can update the goals:

- Are the facilities now accessible to wheelchairs and safe for young children?
- Do the community members now seem more tolerant of people's individual differences?
- Are some community activities now appropriate for people in minority groups?

Some people see reviews as a safeguard that allows them to change their attitudes more radically or with more speed, or to take more risks than if they had no such safeguard. They may be prepared to give integration more of a go if they know that they have a safeguard (a regular review) that allows them to change their approach or to take a step back if they have been too risky or too radical.

Community members have a clear perspective of integration when all the community's policies reflect social justice, and when the integration policy is thus one example of the community's wider attitude. An integration policy indicates the planning, organisation and forethought that the community uses to provide equal chances and choices for all its members.

Chapter Seven

PREPARATION

Integration is happening: people who have a disability are trying more experiences, joining more clubs, working at a wider variety of jobs and meeting more people. However some people are less involved in these situations than they would like; they are spectators rather than participants or they participate in the community's programs but don't belong to the community's social life.

One of the biggest hurdles to integration—to turning attendance into participation, interaction and interdependence—is that people feel inexperienced, uncertain and wary of integration (chapter 4). They feel unprepared. There is certainly no magic formula for the preparation of people for integration. A formula would be impossible to find because people's roles in integration differ, as do their beliefs and concerns, past experiences, motivation, abilities, disabilities and expectations. However preparation for parents, staff, community members and people with a disability can be important for integration's success.

THE GOALS OF PREPARATION

Preparation has three overall goals—to provide information, to teach any necessary skills and to promote attitudes that will help integration work most successfully.

Effective preparation is flexible, specific and individually planned. It may involve formal preparation and sharing of information before the person with a disability arrives, practical on-the-spot learning when the person has arrived and ongoing development of specific skills while the person continues his involvement in the community. Effective preparation involves some 'before' and 'after', some 'formal' and 'informal' but most importantly it is tailored for particular community members and for a specific person who has particular abilities and difficulties.

GENERAL CONSIDERATIONS FOR PREPARATION

Natural learning can be useful. Sometimes the best way to teach about disability and integration is through natural learning when people with a disability attend a community; people may be best educated by example. People are generally not interested in learning things they don't currently need to know, so learning on-the-spot (about the person they can see at activities that are happening) may be more easily remembered than general information about integration. In this way a person with a disability just joins a community as other people do, and any questions are answered as they arise.

Learning on-the-spot may be so subtle and natural that people may not realise they are being educated or prepared for anything. They may have learnt how to use a hammer by watching a neighbour, how to skip a rope by trial and error, how to hang the washing by asking their Grandma, how to kick a football by practising and how to cross the road because lots of people in their community taught them the best way. Likewise they can learn how to work, play, talk with or help a person with a disability by watching, asking, practising, and by being taught the best way as the opportunity arises.

Prior formal preparation can be useful. Sometimes learning on-the-spot is too late. Some people want information and skills before they are faced with integration in order to feel confident and effective.

> *An adult community member*: I went to my boyfriend's house and was introduced to his mother who had the most appalling stutter. I could hardly understand a word she said. I felt humiliated, as I couldn't talk to her, and furious that my boyfriend hadn't warned me in order to reduce my discomfort and his Mum's. Just a few words of preparation would have made all the difference and showed her and me some respect.

> *An adult community member*: As we went into his parent's house, Tim asked me if I knew about his Dad (I remembered his Dad as an intelligent, vigorous man though I hadn't seen him for ten or so years). He explained that his Dad had Alzheimer's disease and would probably say nothing. I was so grateful for this information. I was able to take the lead, shake hands and say a few everyday words. Otherwise I could have embarrassed everyone there by trying to talk to him more and even imagined he was joking with me or being rude by not replying.

Prior preparation for integration (like before a child begins at school or before a group of people who have a disability move into the house next door) may make a big fuss about a normal course of events; it gives a high profile to something which should be straightforward and unremarkable.

Prior preparation may not be as effective as hoped. It not only makes a fuss but it can also be interpreted as asking permission for integration when none is needed. It is not something done when any other person joins a community and therefore is not always appropriate. It may raise more concerns than the fears it is supposed to allay.

Preparation has a purpose. The three different aspects of preparation —knowledge, skills, and attitudes—are intertwined, but preparation can often be more effective if one aspect is identified as the most important for *this* group at *this* time. The format, content and timing of the session needs to be matched to the session's purpose:

- Showing workmates how to lift and transfer a person with a disability may best be done by learning on-the-spot.
- Information about the effects of a head injury on language and learning may be best provided in a discussion prior to the child's arrival at school.
- Helping classmates understand cerebral palsy may best be done by some disability awareness exercises.

Preparation must be relevant.   Different types of information may be wanted by different groups of people and by different individuals within each group. Preparation needs to provide what people want to know and address the concerns they have; this is more likely to be remembered than general information. Examples need to be relevant so people can see integration in relation to themselves and their service, not just in relation to someone else's workplace or childcare centre.

Preparation can include general information.   General information about integration can be important: the nature of integration and normalisation, how and why integration happens and the importance of risks, choices, opportunities, responsibilities and normal expectations (chapters 2 and 3). The best timing for general information about integration will vary according to the particular community's attitudes and to the urgency of their need for specific information.

Preparation includes specific information.   Providing specific information reinforces an important notion about integration and normalisation—that people are individuals. Specific preparation provides information and skills that don't necessarily pertain to spina bifida, but to *this* person with spina bifida. Specific preparation provides information on how to help *this* amputee into a car, how to communicate with *this* particular person who has a head injury, how to help *this* child with Down syndrome concentrate for longer.

An appropriate preparation format is important.   Preparation needs to be presented in a way that carefully informs other people rather than asks their permission. A community's legal right to accept or reject a person with a disability is not an issue for discussion during preparation. People don't ask permission of neighbours before they buy a house, so why should a group of people with a disability do so? It is certainly useful if householders understand their neighbours, and preparation can help them do this. It is also useful if they like their disabled neighbours but it is not vital.

Preparation for integration may be appropriately provided as part of information sessions that already exist for another purpose: lifting techniques and workplace modification can be incorporated into general occupational health and safety lectures at work; individual differences and disability can be incorporated into health and human relations courses at school. By providing preparation in ordinary ways, integration is not seen as anything special; its ordinariness is reinforced.

Preparation sessions about integration in general or about a specific disability may by ineffective unless group members have a particular person with a particular disability in mind. Otherwise general information may just promote the application of an identical program to all people with a disability rather than individual programs based on people's individual needs in individual communities.

Active learning is the best form of preparation. Active learning about disability adds experience and relevance to situations. Knowledge through experience is more easily remembered and used than passive facts and a list of 'dos' and 'don'ts'.

Active learning can be provided through on-the-spot situations. Excellent materials are available that involve active learning about a particular disability through sequential programs that provide information and graded experiences (sometimes called 'disability awareness programs'). They cover a variety of situations and disabilities, and are useful for people with varying levels of experience.

Active learning can include discussion and practice at specific skills (walking with a blind person, talking to a dysarthric person, helping a child with spasticity have a drink) and at problem-solving (workplace layout or planning outings for people who use a wheelchair).

Interaction and interdependence help people develop positive attitudes towards integration. People frequently find that their attitudes change when they have the chance to know someone more closely: they discover that the person isn't a snob but just shy, isn't bossy just lonely. Prejudice can be reduced by increased contact between people who have a disability and other people, particularly if this contact involves interaction and interdependence, not just passive attendance and observation.

> *A teacher:* Through having some hearing impaired students regularly visit my class, my students changed their attitudes. Instead of 'That deaf kid is in the sandpit', they said things like 'It's Jane's turn on the trampoline'.

Increased contact with people who have various disabilities is more likely to lead to attitude change. People with a disability become more familiar; their abilities and ordinariness can be recognised.

> *A workmate:* John does a good day's work and enjoys a beer when we ask him to join us at the pub.

Good preparation sets an example. Preparation sets in motion a process that can support and maintain integration: a process of good communication, of shared information, of planning and evaluation. The provision of preparation indicates that a community is ready to set aside time and effort to make integration work. It is the beginning of a community's acceptance of its responsibility towards people who have a disability, its responsibility to cater for all people equally.

Preparation sets an example in the terms it uses. People can learn to use words that aren't belittling, prejudicing or segregating: 'a house in the community' rather than 'a community residential unit', 'a person with a disability' rather than 'disabled people' and 'water play' or 'swimming lessons' rather than 'hydrotherapy'.

Good preparation is selective.   In any group there will probably be some people who don't believe in or want to know about integration. On the whole preparation is most effective when it is directed at a couple of key people who have shown an awareness of integration and an interest to learn more. Presenting these key people with active learning situations that provide information, skills and an understanding of attitudes helps them be effective in making integration work. In turn, their effective attitudes and skills set an example and demonstrate to other people that integration is a simple concept which can be enhanced by everyone.

> If the teacher is accepting, the kids are accepting.

> *A parent*:   Simon's girlfriend Gail came away on holidays with us and he was very anxious about what she would think of Jane. But Gail was wonderful. It let Simon see Jane with new eyes—the fact that Gail thought Jane was okay meant Simon began to think Jane was okay.

SPECIFIC PREPARATION SITUATIONS

As integration has become more common, people have gained experience in developing different preparation formats that are effective in particular situations. Certainly no two situations are identical—no two staff members or two parents have the same preparation needs; no two communities have identical resources. Nevertheless, there are often issues of common concern to people who play a similar role in the same or in different communities.

COMMUNITY PREPARATION

Information is vital for good community preparation.   Community members deserve to be equally and appropriately informed about integration, no matter what their role. Parents who do volunteer reading at the local school, canteen staff at a workplace, young children and senior staff are all community members who have a part to play in making integration work.

> *A school community member*:   Some parents of children at the local school didn't even know there was a special unit on their school grounds. No-one had thought to mention this in the school promotion brochure or weekly newsletter. Those parents that did know it existed had no idea how it worked or what its relationship was with the rest of the school.

Do community members know why they are seeing more people with a disability in their community? Do they know if the community has an integration policy and a process to follow?

Respect for confidentiality is important. A preschool teacher may need to know a child's diagnosis and its implications, but its relevance to other community members may breach the confidentiality the child's family wishes. It may also label the child in a way that defeats integration. The preschool community may be better prepared by having an understanding of Jane's abilities, likes and dislikes.

In some instances, the use of correct diagnostic terms can stop people using derogatory or prejudiced terms. 'The people living next door to you are not mental. They have an intellectual disability.'

PARENTS OF PEOPLE WITH A DISABILITY

Information is vital for parent preparation. Parents need information about the people who may be involved in the community with their child: their title, roles and skills. What is the difference between an integration teacher and an integration aide? What does a visiting teacher do? Who is the special needs advisor? Is a speech pathologist the same as a speech therapist? What is a personal care attendant? Where do I find an advocate?

In order to put parents on an equal footing with professionals who know all the jargon, parents need information about terms and abbreviations that will be used. What is 'ascertainment'? How does a 'special assistance unit' differ from a 'special education unit'? How do 'cluster houses' differ from 'supported accommodation'? What is the 'least restrictive alternative'? What is a 'work enclave'?

> *A parent*:   She said 'You're child is eligible for V.T., O.T. and regular help from the S.E.U.' and did I think that would be enough. I didn't know what she meant.

Parents want to know about available resources (personnel, equipment, programs, volunteers or grants), about evaluating their suitability and their child's eligibility, and about application procedures. The best way to get information about people, words, abbreviations and resources is to be persistent in asking.

Parent support can provide preparation.   Formal or informal contact between parents can be a source of advice and comfort.

> *A parent*: I was worried about my severely disabled child going to regular school, but another parent whose child had been integrated showed me an article. It said that bullying, abuse and being tricked into harmful activities didn't happen. She'd found it to be true. I was so relieved. I'll be able to tell other parents that our kids aren't as isolated as we think—they make lots of friends with the other kids. I think it's important to pass on this information.

Contact between parents can reassure them that they are not alone in their feelings.

> *A parent*: I felt such public property when Jane went to regular school. Everyone knew her and me. When I met John's mum she said she felt the same.

Understanding the reality of integration is good preparation. What is 'being realistic'? It can mean knowing that there will be good and bad aspects, but that integration is worth a try.

> *A parent*: I never expect too much, so anything good that happens is a bonus.

Being realistic can also mean weighing up the advantages and disadvantages of a situation (chapter 12), making a decision and taking responsibility for it rather than just letting integration happen without having given it a thought.

> *A parent*: I was scared of all that could go wrong, but I knew nothing could be worse than last year's experience at a segregated school.

Being realistic can mean keeping in mind the self-talk (chapter 16) 'Nothing is forever'. Just like choosing a community (chapter 5) no decision need be forever.

PEOPLE WHO HAVE A DISABILITY

People often experience mixed emotions about new situations— excitement about new opportunities, fear of the unknown, longing for familiarity and safety, or worry about acceptance. These feelings may be even more mixed for people with a disability as their confidence may be low in both their ability to fit in and in other people's desire to accept them. Preparation can be used to warn them of what to expect and to help them develop attitudes and skills which will make their integration work.

Does readiness for integration exist? How prepared is prepared enough? Arguments about people being ready for an experience are common, even about people who don't have a disability: 'Are they really ready for marriage?', 'Is she ready to live on her own?'.

Readiness for integration is often discussed on both the part of the person with the disability ('Is he ready for integration?') and on the part of the particular community ('I don't think that school is ready for integration'). Perhaps no-one is ever fully ready for any situation.

> *An adult*: I wasn't ready for single motherhood but you soon get ready when you have to. You're more ready than you think.

> *A parent*: I wasn't ready to be the parent of a disabled child but I was given no choice. It is amazing what you can do when you have to, ready or not.

The idea of 'readiness' can be misused as a reason to postpone or reject integration. People can argue that a person with a disability is not enough like the other people in the community where she's going, and too similar to the people in the community from where she's come. This idea of readiness (that you must be reasonably similar to other community members before you can be allowed to become part of the community and therefore become even more similar) is not very sound. People learn more about a community by being in it than by watching it.

How can you be ready for something you've never experienced? How can you learn the skills needed to manage in a community if you still live in a different community? How can you learn to manage money or to cook if your segregated community buys what you need and cooks your food?

> *A psychologist*: It's as silly as the idea of 'the wetness test' where children are in the pool and you are trying to see if they are ready to get dry. Each time you feel them they don't feel even a little bit dry so you never give them the chance to get dry, but keep them wet where they are more 'at home' with all the other 'wet' people.

Despite concerns about a term like 'readiness', many people believe that some skills make integration more successful. Usually these skills are not based on intelligence or education, but are likely to be social or independence skills.

> *A teacher*: Having reasonably effective communication, not necessarily speech.

> *A club leader*: Being capable of giving and taking, of interacting, not being totally passive or totally aggressive.

> *A teacher*: Being tolerant of the bustle and noise we have here.

> *A teacher*: Having basic classroom skills like attending, concentrating, staying in the seat and staying on task.

> *A volunteer*: Knowing how to ask for help as an equal, rather than not asking at all or asking angrily.

> *A parent*: Respecting his belongings and other people's.

> *A child community member*: I don't like it when other kids interrupt me and stop me working and concentrating.

Readiness can be a useful concept if it is seen as a general tool for planning rather than as an absolute fact. It implies knowing the goals of integration for this person in this community, and the skills/resources/attitudes that are needed and must be 'ready' in order to achieve these goals. If the idea of 'readiness' leads to good planning, it can be useful.

Orientation to the community can be important. Orientation sessions can acclimatise participants to the community (schools, universities and jobs). A longer orientation period may be useful, perhaps when the facilities are empty—a school at a weekend or a job after hours—as well as when they are in normal use. Orientation can involve physical facilities

(Where are the toilets and the canteen?), staff (who do I see about pay or if I feel sick?), equipment (How do I clock on?) and expectations.

Orientation may be in the form of a *trial-period* in the community—perhaps at the swimming club or scouts—before joining and paying the annual dues. This time can be useful for a person with a disability—to work out the best resources, train staff and identify the skills that promote effective integration.

To make best use of a trial period, its purpose and conditions must be clarified beforehand. After the trial period is finished, how and by whom will a decision be made about continued attendance? Is this trial period normally a time when potential members can reject the club? Do the same conditions apply if the person has a disability or not? Does the club see the trial period as an opportunity to accept or reject the applicant, rather than a time to be used for specific planning for his integration?

Some communities have *transition programs* (chapter 8) for individuals moving from one community to another. Others offer 'taster' or 'have-a-go' programs where potential participants can *experience a variety of programs* before committing themselves. This is an example of real choice based on real experience.

Individuality is the basis of preparation.

> *A parent*:   I taught him a few square-dance steps before we went to the dance. That sort of thing always gives him a head start and he has more chance of keeping up.

> *A principal of a special school*:   We teach them the scout pledge and some basic scout skills before we get them into their local pack.

> *An employer*:   I had to teach him lots of slang when he started the job. He didn't know what a 'cup of char' was or what 'hold your horses' meant. We've taught him a lot.

STAFF PREPARATION

It is important that any preparation that is available to staff is available to all staff, not just those most directly concerned with the person who has the disability: all the teachers at the school not just those who teach the child, all the staff even those who work in other sections of the factory.

Information is vital for staff preparation.   Just like the parents of a person with a disability, staff need information about the people who may be involved with integration, the terms and abbreviations that may be used, the resources that are available and any integration processes or policies that will be followed.

In addition, staff need information about the person's individual abilities and difficulties, not just the name of her disability: How visually impaired is she? How much does she stutter? How far can she reach? They also need to know about her experience in similar communities and her expectations: What sort of work experience placements has she had? What does she know about this community?

This information can be gained in a number of ways:

- *Written information* is useful as a record and to confirm other sources of information (particularly verbal instructions or demonstrated techniques), but is not usually sufficient on its own. Staff need to be specific about the sort of written information they want: a description of John's past development, current functioning or most effective communication technique?
- *Verbal information* can be suitable for everyday situations and preferences: 'John likes outdoor play more than indoor play', 'John already knows how to tie a bowline'. Verbal information may not be appropriate for other types of specific information like managing Jane's epileptic fits or transferring her from a car to a wheelchair.
- A *demonstration* can be particularly suitable for showing practical skills: how to help John transfer from the floor to a chair, how to fix the paper so Jane can write effectively or how to present choices.
- *Observation* can be particularly valuable. Meeting John in a familiar setting provides information about his possible functioning in the new setting: previous school, class, work training unit or community residence.

Preparation can provide realistic expectations. In the past, staff members at 'special' communities (special schools, sheltered workshops) were considered 'special' because the people being taught or employed were different and 'special'. Integration challenges the role of both 'special' and 'regular' staff by implying two things.

Integration implies that all staff can be staff to people who have a disability. This is not a particularly new idea in the area of teaching—the mark of a good teacher has always been the ability to teach across a broad range of abilities, interests and levels. What is new is that integration has increased the ranges of the abilities, interests and levels that 'regular' teachers will be teaching.

Integration also implies that the role of 'special' staff will change from one of being solely in charge of 'special' people, to one where the 'special' staff member shares and complements the skills of 'regular' staff.

Preparation can be used to give staff a realistic picture of what is expected: they need not work alone; they are not being 'dumped' with a 'problem'; support personnel and resources are available; they are not expected to make this person 'normal' and they do not have to 'solve' everything, let alone anything!

Preparation can help staff understand differences. Integration situations are not all alike, but many staff who are involved with integration find that some features of their situation are common to other integration situations. Lists always have exceptions, but a list of 'things you may notice' (neither facts nor myths) can be useful in preparing staff for integration:

- A person with a disability may interact more with staff members than other people do—ask for staff help or reassurance more often. She may be used to having staff around and to seeking their help or even receiving their help without asking.
- Staff may find themselves interacting more often with a person who has a disability than they do with other people. People who are different (including disabled) are more obvious, and so catch people's attention more easily. Thus staff may frequently notice and respond to the performance and behaviour of a person with a disability.
- A person with a disability may not 'look busy', not 'look as though he is concentrating', not 'look as though he knows what he is doing'. The facial and body expressions of some people with a disability may not be the same ones that other people use for 'busy', 'concentrating', 'confident' and 'happy'. A person with a disability may not clearly see other people's expressions, or have the muscle control to copy such movements. Also, looking busy when you're not busy (as students seem to learn to do to avoid being given more work!) seems to be a social skill learnt from other children; it may not be easily or quickly learnt by a child who has only recently become involved with children who don't have a disability.
- A person with a disability may not interact as often with other community members (schoolmates and workmates). This may be because she is initiating more interactions with staff than other people are! Maybe staff are initiating more interactions with her. 'Retarded children who get more teacher initiated interactions get less social exchange with their peer group.'[8] Maybe it is because other people are slow to initiate interactions with a person who has a disability.

Specific staff skills may be useful.   Staff often find that being involved with integration puts them in some unfamiliar situations. They may want to develop some new skills in order to be as effective a staff member as they would like, skills (described more fully in chapter 9) such as:

- Setting objectives.
- Planning.
- Task analysis.
- Behaviour modification.
- Using rewards.
- Using cues.
- Working in collaboration with other people.
- Collaborative decision-making.
- Grading programs and experiences.
- Observation and record-keeping.
- Modifying, adapting and providing alternative experiences.
- Using various program formats.

- Promoting interaction among community members.
- Building self-esteem among community members.
- Working with families.
- Developing problem-solving skills.
- Communicating effectively.
- Report writing.
- Programming to help community members generalise skills.

Perhaps the most effective learning about integration *does* take place incidentally, however relevant incidental learning only occurs when there is a minimal degree of acceptance. If people aren't prepared to listen, pay attention, watch and practise then they won't learn to use a hammer, hang the washing, cross a road or kick a football. Neither will they learn how best to interact with other people in their community, whether they have a disability or not. Formal preparation provides a climate where incidental learning by exposure, experience and interaction with people who have a disability *will* happen, and thus where integration *can* happen.

PART THREE: **GO!**

Part three gets integration going for an individual person with particular abilities and difficulties in a specific community.

Integration is unpredictable. Hard work and good intentions do not always make it work, but limited resources, some negative attitudes or a person with very complex disabilities do not always prevent it working either. Although there is no proven formula to make integration 'work' there are a number of factors that are important in maintaining it on a firm footing. They include practical ideas for organising a program, for choosing and using resources and for establishing processes that fulfil the aims of integration.

If a person has severe or multiple disabilities or if a community is inexperienced with integration, then these ideas may need careful consideration. In other circumstances only parts of the information may be directly used, particularly if the person has minimal disabilities or if the community has always welcomed and provided for people with varying abilities and interests.

Programs, resources and processes can provide opportunities for a person to attend a community and participate in its activities; along with appropriate attitudes they can also promote interaction and interdependence among community members. Programs, resources and processes can all get integration going.

Chapter Eight

PARTICIPATION IN A COMMUNITY: PROGRAMS FOR INDIVIDUALS

Communities that successfully meet the needs of members who have a disability also succeed in meeting the needs of all their members. They recognise that members are individuals—they run using different strides, perform better at some school subjects than others, tie their shoelaces in various ways and use different chess strategies. Some members learn by doing, some by listening, some by reading and others by watching and copying.

Communities which recognise these differences among members alter their programs accordingly; they change to meet the needs of members rather than 'working on' them or expecting them to conform to rigid rules. Accordingly, successful communities don't 'work on' a member who has a disability and expect him to become 'more normal' or 'less trouble'. Instead they use processes within their community to help him experience as much as he can of the community's activities in any way he can.

Successful communities individualise their programs to meet the needs of each person while maintaining their uniqueness as a community. A choir is still a choir whether the singers sight-read, memorise the music or use a braille copy, whether they stand to sing, sit on a chair or use a wheelchair.

Individualisation of programs recognises two important aspects of integration—that communities are not static but offer wide experiences and flexibility, and that all people (including all people who have a disability) are different. The program changes made for a member who has a disability may be the same subtle, common alterations made for all members: changes in equipment (an appropriate size and weight tennis racquet), in organisation (sitting near the front of the group if the person is distracted easily) in format or in responsibilities. However more significant changes in program format, content or resources may be needed.

AN INDIVIDUAL PLANNING COMMITTEE

A community has a single community integration committee (chapter 6) but can have a number of **individual planning committees** (individualised program teams), one for each community member who has a disability. Individual planning committees may have different names in different communities: perhaps a 'support group' or an 'integration support group'. They may meet in different ways and the range of their responsibilities may vary. But their role is the same—to provide maximum chances and choices for the person with whom they are concerned within the purpose of the community.

An individual planning committee develops an individual integration program. Each individual planning committee develops an individual integration program for the person with whom it is concerned—a program for the integration of a specific person with particular abilities and difficulties into this community with these resources. The individual integration program is the second part of effective planning for integration which complements the first part (the community's plan for integration [chapter 6]).

In most communities, individualisation of programs is done by staff members: the choirmaster decides the piece of music his madrigal group will learn; the teacher decides how to teach the letters of the alphabet or Newton's laws of gravity; the swimming coach decides when and how to teach a racing dive.

Staff have resources available to help them individualise their programs: the choirmaster seeks advice from other madrigal choirmasters and uses a graded book of madrigal songs; the teacher uses textbooks and the advice of other senior teachers; the coaching manual identifies the pre-requisites for a racing dive and the individual variations on the dive that are acceptable. If a community member has a disability, extra or specific resources may be needed in order to individualise the community's programs or to implement the individualised program. The community's staff do not usually do this alone. Instead, an individual planning committee develops an individual integration program and then identifies and co-ordinates resources to best implement it.

An individual planning committee needs appropriate membership. The committee should include people who:

- Clearly know the person with the disability. (This can actually be the person who has the disability.)
- Clearly know the community including its integration policy, current programs and resources.
- Know about setting objectives.
- Know about planning, modifying and evaluating programs to meet overall goals and specific objectives.

Committees sometimes include additional people for short periods, people whose skills and knowledge complement the skills of regular committee members in relation to specialised areas (like computers or wheelchair access). It is important that the committee doesn't just include 'managers' or 'bosses'. It must include the people who are there where and when integration is happening: the person who has the disability (or someone representing her interests) and the staff who have most contact with her. These are the people whose attitudes and decisions can make integration work.

Committees vary in size. One may only include a couple of people: the parents of a physically disabled girl and a swimming coach; or a person with a disability and the owner of a factory where he has applied for a job. Others include representatives from all the levels of people that are involved with integration in that community. A committee at a worksite may include a vocational counsellor, business owner, union representative, person with the disability and parents; a committee at a school may include a school principal, class teacher, parent, parent advocate, integration aide and specialist teacher.

An individual planning committee makes decisions. Integration is best encouraged if the person who would normally make a decision (parent, staff member or the person himself) does so; integration can be defeated if the most 'ordinary' person is not allowed to make everyday decisions. Individual planning committees work best when it is clear to everyone which sorts of decisions are 'committee decisions' and which are 'on-the-spot' decisions. Some decisions about the program are reasonably made by the committee: how best to use the available resources or which program/group/class/housing arrangement is most appropriate. Many on-the-spot decisions need to be made too. If a person has many staff working with her the staff member in charge of the ordinary community—the teacher at the regular school not the visiting one from the special school, the boss at the workplace trial not the trainer from the training centre—should have the final say about on-the-spot decisions.

AN INDIVIDUAL INTEGRATION PROGRAM

Individualisation of programs should work from strengths and abilities and build on skills. It should relate to personal interests and experiences, provide active participation in learning and encourage interaction among community members.

Each individual planning committee develops in **individual integration program**—a term for the unique combination of all the community's programs which have been individualised for the needs of a particular person with a disability. (The program may be unnamed, or it may have a different name such as individual education program or individual program plan.) The committee applies the four principles of integration (social justice, equal opportunity, non-categorisation and non-segregation) to the community's existing programs: to the school's classroom programs and to their voluntary programs like school play and student council; to the swimming club's training, competition and social programs. The committee then individualises these community programs to meet the person's needs and provide the maximum chances and choices within the community.

Some committees develop their individual integration program by documenting an overall plan and a day-to-day program. The committee:

- Collects information.
- Develops overall goals and priorities.
- Identifies specific objectives.
- Implements an effective day-to-day program.
- Reviews the individual integration program.

INFORMATION COLLECTION

Information is needed about the community. The information needed about the community should be available in the community's integration policy (chapter 6)—an overview of integration as it applies to this community and a list of existing community resources: programs, staff, equipment and community networks.

Information is needed about the person who has the disability. An individual planning committee needs information about a particular person not about a disability: it needs up-to-date information not old opinions or generalisations. Committee members can get this information by talking to people who know the person with the disability well, not just those who are supposed to know him (and certainly not those who know 'someone just like him')! They can talk to people at other communities in which he has been involved: schools, clubs and workplaces.

Assessment can provide some information about the person's abilities and difficulties but the role of assessment in integration is complex and confusing. Assessment is only useful for program planning if an appropriate person does an appropriate form of assessment that provides wanted information and if the information is used. Community-referenced assessment (assessment of a person's actual abilities and needs in a particular community) often provides this (chapter 17).

ESTABLISHMENT OF OVERALL GOALS AND PRIORITIES

Identified goals are important. Some people think that goals for integration aren't needed. They think that a person with a disability joins a community for the same reasons as other people—to belong and to get what she can out of the community: an education at school, a wage at work, increased sporting skills at the basketball club. This is probably true, but a person with a disability may have more specific or additional goals. She may have minor goals on the way to the major goals and the way to reach the goals may not be as clear as it is for other people.

When any person joins a community his goals are not always obvious. He may join an aerobics club to get fit or to lose weight, as a diversion or for a bet; he may have won a free subscription or he may lust after the aerobics instructor! When a person with a disability joins a community his goals may be similar to those of other community members or he may have different goals or different priorities. 'A teenage girl in a wheelchair may join a youth club for the same reasons as other teenagers (to make friends, participate in social outings and go on camps) or for the particular reason of meeting teenagers who don't have a disability. She may also join to consciously participate in the club's social service efforts, as she may have often been on the 'receiving' end of assistance, but never on the 'giving' end.' (chapter 5)

The goals for a person with a disability are qualitatively different in a regular community to those that would be established for her in a special community—the resources are different, the opportunities are different and it is because they *are* different that integration has been suggested.

Common goals and priorities are important.   Different people on the individual planning committee may perceive the goals of integration differently. Their role with integration may influence their perspective, as may their experiences and knowledge of integration (chapter 4). The person with the disability—an important member of the individual planning committee—may know why he wants to join a particular community, and which overall goals or specific objectives would best help him become part of that particular community. If his experience has been mainly in segregated communities, it may be hard for him to know the choices available in the regular community, let alone make a choice from among them. However he may have a clear idea of his priorities from among the overall goals, once they have been established.

Discussion and sharing of information among members of the individual planning committee helps them reach a common decision about goals and priorities. Shared goals encourage sharing of the responsibility for integration; common goals and priorities are important to successful integration (chapter 17).

Goals and objectives relate to a specific person's requirements in a particular community.   Choosing objectives and goals that are relevant to *this* person in *this* community—community-referenced goals and objectives (chapter 17)—is an important ingredient in the success of integration. Common sense often indicates appropriate goals but sometimes information from assessments is used.

Beware of choosing goals just because they are easy to identify, to program and to measure; they may be unrealistic or a low priority for the person with whom the committee is concerned. Competence in practical skills is easy to measure so practical goals are easy to write: tying shoelaces, giving change, using a word processor or learning to swim. Practical skills make a person able to *do* but not necessarily to choose, differentiate between choices, weigh up the pros and cons, argue, challenge, question or answer. Social goals and objectives (to share a toy, wait your turn, assert your rights) may be difficult to identify, program and measure, but they may be more important for interaction and interdependence between community members.

IDENTIFICATION OF SPECIFIC OBJECTIVES

Objectives relate to an overall goal.   An objective is a statement describing how to reach a particular goal. If the overall goal at basketball is improving John's fitness, the specific community-referenced objectives may be:

- John plays in a team for 5 minutes without loss of pace.
- John shoots goals in practice for 10 minutes without rest.
- John's heartrate after the match returns to normal within 5 minutes.

If the overall goal at basketball had been widening John's circle of friends, the specific objectives may have been:

- John identifies 5 of the team members after 6 games.
- John knows 2 life interests of 3 team members by the end of the season.
- John can organise the end of season celebration (or commiseration!) outing.

Objectives are clearly written.   Some objectives are easy to identify— 'learning to fasten her bike helmet' or 'using the bike stand at school' within the goal of 'riding a bike'. Sometimes people suggest objectives that are too vague to be useful—'learning to eat more neatly' or 'communicating what she wants'. Clear objectives include information on *who* will do *what*, under *what conditions, how well* and by *when*. The value of specific objectives is that they provide a place to start (program content), they indicate a way to work towards the objective (program format) and they allow progress to be measured. Progress can be measured because there is an objective to progress towards: Did John's heartrate return to normal after 5 minutes? Can Jane fasten her bike helmet?

Objectives simplify program updating because they are easily broadened or extended within the goal: playing in the team for *10 minutes* without loss of pace or knowing the names of *ten* club members. Clearly written objectives are vital in evaluating the effectiveness of an individual integration program (chapter 17).

IMPLEMENTATION OF AN EFFECTIVE DAY-TO-DAY PROGRAM

Specific objectives indicate appropriate curriculum for an effective day-to-day program. Curriculum is not a word that just applies to schools, subjects or lessons. It means the arrangement of all the experiences or programs being offered by the community—the combination of program content, program format and program resources.

The individual planning committee groups objectives and matches them to the content, format and resources of the community's existing programs. They select, alter and add to the community's programs to individualise them. An effective day-to-day program results from combining the most suitable of the community's programs once they have been individualised for the needs of the person with the disability.

Sometimes the individual planning committee finds that the changes needed in the community's programs would make interaction with other community members very difficult; that attendance at the community is possible, but integration is not. The committee may then decide that a particular objective can't be met in this community, although it remains a valid objective for the person and will hopefully be met in some other community.

PROGRAM CONTENT

Program content is the knowledge and skills available through the subjects and experiences offered.

The community's existing program content may be appropriate. Existing experiences, opportunities and programs may meet most of an individual integration program's objectives. Many objectives are met when a person with a disability is in the community, experiencing its choices, variety, risks and responsibilities.

Not all people learn identical skills from the same experiences; some learn social skills, some learn facts, and some remember less detail than others. If a person recalls less program content, it doesn't necessarily mean that the program content should be changed; it may mean that evaluation of the person's progress may need to be changed.

Consider modifying existing program content. The same subjects or tasks may be used for all community members but the expected skill level or the relative importance of skills may differ for a person with a disability. In woodwork, care of the woodwork tools and learning how to sand with the grain of the wood may be more important than the woodwork item produced or than making a pencil box. In preschool storytime, sitting still and recalling the main story line may be appropriate for some members, whereas using logical thought to extend the story line may be relevant for others.

Regardless of the actual task or subject, a person's objective may be to take turns, to communicate clearly or to keep his attention focused on the task. The program content must allow opportunities for these skills to be practised and reinforced.

Consider adding program content. Sometimes a person needs some program content that other community members don't need. He may lack some pre-requisite skills that are necessary for him to participate in the community's current programs—perhaps he couldn't experience previously used program formats, or illness may have caused infrequent program attendance. Program content will need to be added for him to develop the pre-requisite skills.

Consider alternative or non-traditional program content.   A person may need to learn a 'zero order skill'—a skill that is unnoticed when present and not normally 'taught' at all (like blowing your nose, saying hello or paying attention). Other needed skills may not normally be available as a program in that community though they may be available as program content in other communities: assertion skills, efficient study skills, or interpersonal problem-solving. Non-traditional skills may be taught as a separate program but can be practised and reinforced within the community's broader programs.

PROGRAM FORMAT

Program format is the grouping and presentation of program content—how it is taught. The best program formats match objectives to opportunities that occur frequently and naturally in the community. If the program format is community-referenced, it can use everyday experiences and cues that are available simply because a person attends the community; the program format is obvious—when the experiences happen, they are used. So, *community-referenced assessment* ('she can't recognise coins') identifies specific *community-referenced objectives* ('she needs to recognise coins to buy her lunch in the milkbar') which are best taught through *community-referenced instruction* ('she can buy goods in the community'). This is real-life learning as it happens; the relevance of the objective is obvious and the instruction is natural.

The community's existing program format may be suitable.   The existing program may neatly match the person's objectives—the basketball club may already provide goal shooting sessions that can be used to increase John's fitness. The community itself may provide community-referenced instruction that teaches, reinforces and maintains the community-referenced objectives. If you can't recognise a 50c piece, fit a coin in a slot, push through the turnstile or get your bathing suit on (community-referenced assessment leading to community-referenced objectives) then waiting hot and tired outside the pool is good motivation to learn and practise these things (with the other people providing community-referenced instruction as they use coins and put on their bathing suits).

Consider individually tailoring program attendance time.   Some people with a disability find it difficult to belong and be accepted unless they attend the community and its programs for the same time as other community members. However *part-time attendance* (school for short days, work for two days per week, less days at camp, at the dance for half the evening) can be useful for some people. The committee may find that part-time attendance allows a person to participate at his best because of reduced stamina or health. Don't presume, however, that he won't manage a full day/full week/all evening/on his own without actually trying.

Part-time attendance may take the format of a *social visit*—attendance at

Community-referenced assessment

Community-referenced objectives

Community-referenced instruction

Success

a community for a short period usually with only limited participation expected. Social visits (particularly if program content is inappropriate) may only emphasise differences and perpetuate discrimination. A social visit to a school is often for 'away from the desk' subjects like physical education, music or art. Such subject's social opportunities and program content may not meet objectives for a person with a disability; they may not foster strengths or encourage interaction.

An individual planning committee may consider *shared attendance* (really two part-time attendances) between a special and an ordinary community. Some people consider shared attendance unacceptable—it doesn't offer the reduced physical demands of a single part-time attendance and the person may feel like a visitor at both communities, not be really part of either community. It can be confusing—two sets of friends and staff, two environments, different routines and curriculum—and a person may miss out on some program content because the two settings provide it when she isn't there.

> *A parent*:   At one school the letter of the week was P, and at the other school it was L. This is a child who needs lots of practice to learn anything, and yet he was getting totally confused—less practice at any one thing than the other kids.

However shared attendance works well for some individuals.

> *A parent*:   Shared enrolment was good because it gave the school time to breathe. They had John for two days and then had the rest of the week to plan for the next two days. They weren't so overwhelmed with John and could see his good points rather than just what hard work he was. I also thought it gave John a chance to gradually develop some new friends at the regular school without a sudden complete change of schools.

Some people believe that shared attendance between a special and a regular community *can* work if it is part of a transition period—if there is a clear goal of full-time attendance in the regular community. They believe that shared attendance is acceptable as part of the path towards integration, but not as a goal in itself.

An individual planning committee may consider *increased attendance time* at a particular community. By attending two basketball groups— 'beginners' and 'under-10'—a child may learn the rules faster and get more practice. A committee may consider *delayed attendance*—a person with a disability joining the community after the usual starting time for new members. This can give staff more time to spend with the person who has the disability because other community members are already settled. However a delayed start can make a person seem different and make her integration more difficult. Learning the rules at the same time as other community members may be easier than learning the rules when the other members already know them, and when staff reminders are less frequent.

Transition programs help a person become familiar with the community to which he is going: from a segregated to a regular community, from a junior area to a senior area (brownies to girl scouts) or from one regular community to another (school to work). The transition program may include part-time or shared attendance and often orientation sessions to the physical surroundings, staff, equipment and expectations (chapter 7).

Consider an individual timetable.   Particular types of program format can be used to compensate for dificulties in the community's timetable. *Self-paced* programs—materials used at a person's own rate—may be suitable if health or transport problems make regular program use difficult, or if a person only participates in part of a program and so wants a faster work pace than other group members.

Consider individual learning styles.   *One-to-one* teaching may allow a person to be taught a skill in a specific way with the undivided attention of staff. *Small group* teaching may be appropriate for teaching some skills but not others, or to teach variations on a familiar skill. *Active learning* may suit a person who learns best by 'doing' and 'experiencing', rather than 'watching' and 'being told'.

Mixed-ability groups can avoid comparisons of people's abilities and difficulties. They allow program flexibility because each person works at their own level within the group's variety of levels. Other group members (through *peer tutoring, cross-age tutoring* or *co-operative learning* [chapter 11]) can often explain an activity, and put it in context easily and with more relevance than can staff.

Self-teaching programs are suitable if a person works well with structured material or at times that are awkward to program with staff. Such programs can match an objective like developing increased independence at tasks. They can also be useful when a person needs a program format that is quite different to the format used by other community members (perhaps computer assisted learning); they can program for his needs while not disadvantaging other community members. However alternative program formats can isolate a person from other community members rather than encourage his interaction and interdependence with them.

Non-graded programs can be useful when variety and richness are the basis of the program, not progress made or a grade passed.

Consider adding or modifying practice.   Some people need more practice, or different types or patterns of practice: frequent short practice opportunities or one step at a time.

Some objectives are vital to integration's success (keyboard skills to allow more competitive academic output, or co-ordination skills to allow more involvement at play) and so quick mastery of them may be a high priority. Increased practice can be provided by increased attendance time or through using two communities: keyboard skills taught through fingering games at school plus typing skills at night school, co-ordination taught by ball activities at school and individual therapy out of hours.

Additonal or modified instruction may be needed.   Some people learn best with a full explanation of the task, perhaps with frequent instructions. They may need not just verbal instructions but instructions using all body senses—incorporating doing, touching, seeing, experiencing and hearing. A person may learn best through particular senses or particular instruction formats—he may need cassettes rather than books, diagrams instead of written instructions.

Consider specific rewards.   Enjoyment through participation and success in an activity may be reward enough, but particular types of additional rewards may most appropriately match particular objectives: a new pair of scissors when the objective of sharing art and craft equipment has been met, a basketball goal ring when balance and co-ordination therapy has been completed without complaint.

Consider generalising the skill.   Some people easily generalise skills— apply a skill learnt in one situation to a variety of other situations. Other people need specific programs or cues to help them broaden their skill use: clearing the table in Homecrafts also means doing so after eating at home and after an outside barbecue: looking at the teacher while talking to him at school also means looking directly at the Little Athletics coach.

PROGRAM RESOURCES

Effective programs are developed in response to specific objectives and consider both program content and program format. The program is implemented using resources. The availability of resources may influence the program's content and format, but specific use of resources follows decisions about the content and format. Content, format and resources are intertwined.

Choosing and using appropriate resources is an important facet of successful integration, and is discussed fully in chapter 9.

REVIEW OF AN INDIVIDUAL INTEGRATION PROGRAM

A regular review of an individual integration program provides information so that the program continues to be effective. (It is the program that is being evaluated, not the process of integration in the community nor the person's performance—chapter 17.) A review may indicate that some objectives have been more easily met than others; their common elements can indicate both a person's and a program's strengths, and thus indicate changes in program content or format that also allow more difficult objectives to be met. A regular review also checks a program's continued compliance with the principles of integration: social justice, equal opportunity, non-categorisation and non-segregation.

PROGRAM CHECKLIST

An individual integration program is developed in response to goals, priorities and objectives, so a review is tied to them. A program checklist chart (p 88) can be used for *each* objective developed by the individual planning committee to check the appropriateness and ongoing relevance of program content and formats. (A checklist for program resources is on p 103.)

List the objective.   The objective may, of course, be identical to other community member's objectives (a school maths program to learn fractions) or it may differ (a youth club's social service program to provide the opportunity to give assistance rather than always receive it).

Was this objective identified by community-referenced assessment?
Is the objective related to the needs of *this person* in *this community?*
Learning to use a bus timetable may increase some people's opportunities
for independence, but it is not a community-referenced objective for a
person in a wheelchair who can't use a bus. Learning to stack an increasing number of small blocks indicates development of eye-hand co-
ordination, but is rarely a community-referenced skill used in play, work or
life.

What is this objective's term of relevance?   Is the objective of life-long
relevance (like learning to tidy up when a task is finished)? Will it be
relevant for the term of this person's involvement in this community (walking in a 'crocodile' at primary school) but not necessarily for the whole of
her life? Is it of short-term use?

Does this objective actively support this person's integration?   Does
the objective promote this person's integration or just discourage her
segregation? Is it a 'zero order' skill? Zero order skills (unnoticed when
present but their absence is noticed) can help prevent segregation and
categorisation though they rarely promote integration. However by preventing categorisation and segregation they can allow more social contact to
occur. Other objectives support 'expected' goals—goals all people are
expected to eventually learn (like knowing the time or handling money).
Some skills are highly valued (like using a computer or running a
marathon) and can provide status; they promote integration, not just prevent segregation and categorisation.

Is this program content the least restrictive?   Do the program content
and the objectives encourage this person's maximum participation in this
community? Learning to use a taxi may provide some opportunities, but
learning to use public transport may provide more opportunities. Is this
objective appropriate to the person's age and status; will it enhance her
social image? Setting inappropriate objectives defeats integration. An adult
with an intellectual disability learning to build a sandcastle does little for
his image or status; learning to set the fireplace does more.

Is this program format the least restrictive?   Is the program format
the least 'different', most 'ordinary', least intrusive format? Is program
advice or support offered to existing staff before additional staff are sought,
or before the person with the disability is withdrawn for 'special' teaching?
Is the format appropriate to this person's age and status; will it enhance his
social image? Learning skills through inappropriate means defeats integration. An adult can learn to pour using a kitchen skills program (an
appropriate program format) or though play in a sandpit (an inappropriate
format). Sandpit play does not enhance his social image or give him
appropriate practice.

PROGRAM CHECKLIST

Date. . . . . .   Client name. . . . .

OBJECTIVE

. . . .
. . . .
. . . .
. . . .

OBJECTIVE IS COMMUNITY-REFERENCED	this person [ ]	this community [ ]	
OBJECTIVE HAS RELEVANCE	short-term [ ]	life of this community [ ]	life-long [ ]
OBJECTIVE SUPPORTS INTEGRATION	zero order skill [ ]	'expected' goal [ ]	high status skill [ ]
PROGRAM CONTENT IS LEAST RESTRICTIVE	age [ ]	status [ ]	opportunities [ ]
PROGRAM FORMAT IS LEAST RESTRICTIVE	age [ ]	status [ ]	resource use [ ]
COMMUNITY-REFERENCED INSTRUCTION IS USED	to teach skill [ ]	to reinforce skill [ ]	to maintain skill [ ]

REVIEW DATE   . . / . . / . . . .

Does this program maximise the use of community-referenced instruction? Can these objectives be taught, reinforced and maintained by natural circumstances in the community? Do natural situations occur frequently to provide enough practice to maintain the objective? Greeting people is a skill which is used frequently, whereas learning to sing 'Happy Birthday' is not used often. Handling money in a pretend situation or at an adult centre canteen allows less community participation than using real money to buy real goods in a real shop in a real street.

What is the date of the program review? Effective programs are regularly reviewed to maintain their effectiveness.

An individual integration program is a tool used to help reach the goal of successful integration. Don't let 'sticking to the program' become a substitute goal for 'successful integration'. The program should be flexible, outline the possibilities and prepare for the difficulties, but primarily, the program should help integration work.

Chapter Nine

APPROPRIATE RESOURCES

Social justice stresses that all people have equal value and the same rights, but recognises that people use different means to achieve those rights. Some people need particular resources so that they can participate equally; without resources, a person with a disability may be denied the chances and choices that integration should provide.

Resources for integration broadly fall into three groups: human resources, equipment resources and resource services. They are used by an individual planning committee to help implement an individual integration program. The availability of resources may influence the program's content and format, but specific use of them follows decisions about the content and format. Content, format and resources are intertwined.

Resources can help integration work but they can't ensure that integration happens. A particular resource can help a person attend her local community and participate in its programs (particular scissors may let John cut more accurately; a specific wheelchair may let Jane fit under the science workbench more easily). However they can't ensure equal participation or the same rights, responsibilities and respect for all community members. Interaction and interdependence between community members happens through community members' attitudes, not through resources.

RESOURCE FALLACIES

Some communities believe that enough resources or the right resources will solve the 'integration problem'. They think integration works just by obtaining the right pair of scissors, a different type of wheelchair, a more suitable integration aide, visiting specialist staff 'who do their job properly' or a different maths program. They may think that:

Integration always needs resources. Some communities use 'Not enough resources are available' as a reason to postpone integration or as a way of preventing a person with a disability joining their community. Such discrimination against a minority group, based on lack of resources, denies social justice. Resources can make attendance at a community easier or interaction more likely, but integration does not always need resources.

Some objectives can only be reached if particular resources are tied to them. The availability of resources sometimes makes it easier to reach a particular objective; a particular type of resource may be most suitable. But other ways and other resources can usually be found.

All people with a particular disability need particular resources. —'Spina bifida children always need an integration aide.'—Some people with a particular type of disability need a particular type of resource (some, but not all, blind people need a brailler), but the best resources are based on the needs of individual people. One child with a hearing impairment needs more integration aide time but less equipment than another child; a cup that suits one person with hemiplegia doesn't suit another.

A person needs the same resources in all communities. —'The resources Jane needs in the classroom are the same resources she needs on camp.'—Some people need a particular resource in most communities (a wheelchair) but the best resources are community-referenced—based on needs in individual communities.

A particular person will need this level of resource or type of resource indefinitely. —'The resources Jane needs in primary school are the same resources she will need at high school.'—The best resources only remain 'best' if they are reviewed regularly and change along with the person's changing needs.

Resources can always be used in other situations or with other people. The best resources are community-referenced, so they relate to a specific person's current needs in a specific community not to past needs, future needs, imagined needs or someone else's needs!

There must be a resource to help this person. Sometimes the best people, equipment and services are not the solution to a difficulty; they are only the best available response to the difficulty. Resources don't guarantee integration will work; integration doesn't guarantee success or happiness; integration only guarantees the chance to try.

If resources are available, they must be needed and we must get them. —'We'd better grab them before everyone else.'—Resources that help integration work are individually prescribed.

More is better. More equipment, staff and advice–more resources won't 'solve integration', and in fact they can add to the 'integration problem' through the worry of finding, funding and co-ordinating them: equipment may not increase independence if a person becomes passively dependent on it; a child may not learn to express his needs or make choices if an adult is always available to anticipate his needs and choices; 'hovering specialists' are only useful if they respond to a resource need.

More is not better

'Special' is better. Special equipment, special programs, specially trained staff–'special' resources can lead to a person being labelled 'different'; a full-time integration aide's presence can hamper spontaneous involvement of a child with her peers; dependence on a 'special' cup can limit a child's ability to manage with a variety of cups.

Resources can stop the parents of other community members complaining about integration here. Equipment or an integration aide may help dispel some fears about integration: its effect on teacher time or fears about safety (chapter 4). These resources may not directly relate to a particular person's needs, but if they allow a community to be more receptive and thus develop more positive attitudes towards integration, then they may be appropriately prescribed; they relate to a person's 'particular community.'

THE 'BEST' RESOURCES

Fortunately most communities realise that resources alone are not a solution to integration; they also realise that appropriately chosen and appropriately used resources can be *part of a process* that makes integration able to happen, makes it more possible and makes it likely to work.

The 'best' resources are only best at a particular time—for one person attending a particular community and participating in a particular program. The 'right suburb for everyone' doesn't exist and neither does the 'best community for integration' or the 'best resources for integration'. Resources are only as good as the reasons for which they are chosen and as the ways in which they are used.

Resource needs must be clearly identified and communicated. Community-referenced objectives identify the resources needed to implement the program's content and format. Clearly stating resource needs helps define the most suitable type of resource and thus helps a community obtain the best resource.

- 'We need some way of helping John hold a camera.'
- 'We would like a program of "work hardening" as John is starting work as a storeman and packer in 6 weeks.'
- 'We would like someone to work with Jane in the reading program each morning for 15 minutes.'
- 'We need a typewriter, and also advice about which brand to buy and how to introduce it.'
- 'We need advice about communicating with Jane, particularly about how to offer her choices. What do we do if she won't use her communication board?'

Even if resource needs are clear, obtaining resources that give the right help at the right time is not always easy. Sometimes the available resources (particularly the human resources) don't or can't provide help when and how it is needed: an integration aide may be available at preschool but not as often as needed; a program development assistant may be unavailable for another 6 months; a consultant therapist may only provide a service to staff, or, conversely, only be available to work with the person who has the disability.

This situation will never change unless specific resource needs and their rationale are made clear. If the objective behind the resource need is clarified, the program development assistant may be able to provide a general program to use until time is available to look at specific needs, or the consultant therapist may be able to work as requested—with the person who has the disability, with staff or with both.

Resources must be carefully chosen. Identification of resource needs and recognition of resource fallacies provides information about choosing resources.

- 'More' resources are not 'better' resources.
- 'Special' resources are not 'better' resources.

- The best resources are chosen to match the needs of a particular person.
- The best resources are chosen to match a person's needs in a particular community (community-referenced assessment). A person does not need the same resource in all communities.
- The best resources are matched to objectives in an individual integration program.
- The best resources are the least restrictive resources.

Resources must be carefully used.   Identification of resource needs and recognition of resource fallacies also provides information about using resources.

- The best resources complement program content and format.
- The best resources complement other resources.
- The best resources are regularly reviewed to match changes in the person and the community.
- The best resources are used in the least restrictive way—allowing maximum chances, choices, learning and development.

HUMAN RESOURCES

Specific objectives help define resource needs and thus the most suitable human resource. They provide an initial job role and can be used to evaluate and to modify the job role, and to clarify the person's relationship to other service providers. Is the resource person required to assess or assist the person who has the disability, consult with staff, provide a specific program, plan objectives, teach objectives or prepare materials? What is the relationship of the resource person to staff, volunteers, committees, outside 'specialist' staff, the parents of the child and people in the community? Who is in charge and to whom is this person responsible?

CHOOSING HUMAN RESOURCES

Applying the least restrictive alternative (chapter 3) to available human resources helps identify the most appropriate human resource:

Use existing staff.   A person with a disability is entitled to an equal share of regular staff time; this time can be carefully and effectively used. Trained or untrained staff within the community can be re-organised to meet resource needs: staff members may have prior experience in grading programs or evaluating equipment; clerical staff could teach typing and ground staff help implement work hardening skills; the regular assistant at a school or preschool could assist with the reading program.

> An unexpected byproduct (of mixed ability groups) is a more economic deployment of staff and the ability to develop untapped staff interests and qualifications. The single most wasted resource in secondary education is the unused creativity of teachers.[9]

Use community members. The people within a community are often the best, most available and most flexible resource. Paired acitivities, peer tutoring or buddy systems can provide a human resource in the least restrictive way. All the community's members can learn to communicate with Jane once information is available. Other community members can be a valuable resource for modelling social interaction and acceptable behaviour, and for reinforcement of skills.

Use volunteers. The community may already use volunteers in many ways: on excursions, for maintenance tasks or for small group activities. Using volunteers may be the way the community most often gains additional human resources, a more ordinary way than using 'special' outside help.

Use community-referenced instruction. (Chapter 8) People in the wider community can be unknowing volunteers, be a pool of human resources providing community-referenced instruction through natural circumstances and consequences.

Use ordinary resources in the wider community. Shops, offices and public facilities may have training programs: a 'shop assistant's code of ethics', a 'job specification for storepersons'. Their staff may be able to modify their programs to specific requirements or provide training in the natural setting.

Use resource services. (p 98) Experienced resource personnel may provide a variety of services: assessment, program development, task analysis, small group or individual work, advice or information. But, 'outside specialist help' or 'additional specific help' may not be the most flexible resource.

Advertise and employ a person. Advertising can attract a person with the exact skills needed. This may provide a more suitable human resource than using people from a resource service who may be limited in the roles they perform.

HUMAN RESOURCES FOR IN-SERVICE

Staff, parents and community members all form part of the community; preparation and ongoing education about integration helps provide them with information, skills and attitudes that can help make integration work. The best preparation and education reflects the real needs of these community members, not just what management thinks they need or what is easily provided. Some people want specific information about a particular person: his preferences, habits, humour—all the things that make him individual. Staff often want information about specific techniques and strategies that will help them feel more effective:

- *Setting objectives*—particularly in relation to areas like behaviour or motivation.
- *Planning* the best use of time and resources.
- *Task analysis* to enable goal-directed, step-by-step teaching.
- *Behaviour modification*—setting behavioural objectives, recording behaviour and appropriately using rewards.
- *Using rewards*—choosing the right rewards, changing, replacing or fading them.
- *Using cues*—choosing the right cues, changing, replacing or fading them.
- *Working in collaboration* with other people or providing leadership and direction to support staff.
- *Collaborative decision-making* as a model for involving families and other professionals.
- *Grading programs and experiences*—gradually decreasing or increasing the difficulty of programs and experiences.
- *Modifying, adapting and providing alternative experiences and activities*, particularly when an experience or situation is inaccessible to a particular person.
- *Observation and record-keeping* for documenting programs and behaviour changes, and for precision teaching.
- *Using specific program formats*, like co-operative learning tasks or peer tutoring.
- *Promoting interaction and interdependence* among community members.
- *Building self-esteem* in community members.
- *Working with families*—understanding family systems and dynamics.
- *Developing problem-solving skills* among community members.
- *Developing problem-solving skills* for themselves!
- *Programming to increase responsibilities and choices* for community members.
- *Communicating effectively.*
- *Report writing.*
- *Programming to generalise skills* for community members.

HUMAN RESOURCE NETWORKS

Ongoing education can help staff feel recognised and supported, particularly if their interactional needs are also met through a network of people with similar needs.

Staff burnout may not be caused by the extra demands of a community member who has a disability or by extra meetings. Staff burnout and stress is more often related to feeling a lack of support, worth and recognition. Staff often say that they want 'support' but the type of support they actually want varies. Some find that the provision of resources helps them feel supported by the community and by management. Other staff want increased knowledge and skills through ongoing education. Some staff want support from other staff members at their community.

> *A teacher*: I want other teachers to understand my position. I want other teachers to share the responsibility. Okay, I'm his teacher but he's our responsibility as a school.

Some staff want support from staff in a similar position to themselves but in other communities. A 'staff support network' can be a major step towards providing this support, particularly if management acts positively by providing time for release of staff or financial assistance to attend network meetings. Such networks may be role specific: a teacher network, an integration aide network or a network for staff working in supported employment. Such networks may have an information focus and thus assume a role of staff education, or they may have a problem-sharing focus or be a lobby group with a political role.

EQUIPMENT RESOURCES

Equipment—tools, utensils, furniture and materials—can be an invaluable resource, but 'Let's get newer/bigger/special/more/different equipment' should certainly not be the first reaction to a difficulty. Apply the least restrictive alternative to assist with equipment choice:

Consider different techniques to achieve independence before using equipment. Seek new ways of achieving independence and reduce the need for equipment by using task analysis, ideas in books, advice from people at resource services or resource networks: Jane may be able to identify her bag hook if it is the one nearest the door rather than a centrally placed one that has to be tactually or visually identified; John may not need special scissors, but instead need a different cutting technique—perhaps holding the paper flat and over the edge of the table rather than in the air; Jane may not need a complicated device to hold the nail upright while she hammers if she can be shown how to use 'Blue Tac' to keep it upright on its own; John may need specific instructions about marking the pattern onto the wood instead of a template.

Modify or improve existing equipment before buying new equipment. Jane may not need a new wheelchair to fit under the chemistry bench if the bench's facing board is cut away or a slide-out tray is fitted under the bench. John may not need new scissors if the current ones are sharpened.

Choose versatile equipment. Use each piece of equipment fully: a standing frame can be used indoors and outdoors, at morning tea, at tabletop tasks and at the painting easel. A non-slip place mat on the table stops all the crockery from slipping and is easier than gluing a non-slip surface under each crockery piece or limiting a person to one piece of adapted crockery.

Choose commercially available well designed equipment before equipment designed specifically for people who have a disability. A particular commercially available cup may be just as suitable as a 'special' one. Are commercially available 'magnetic blocks' easier to hold than Lego? A solid colour or dark rimmed dinner set may be easier to see (and thus to use and lay out) than one with complex visual detail. Chess pieces with knobs may be easier to use than small ones. Maybe John doesn't need special spring-loaded scissors or an easier cutting technique, but instead needs good quality commercially available scissors.

RESOURCE SERVICES

Resource services are service available to communities to assist them with integration. They can often provide flexible, individually prescribed resources. They usually respond only to requests (and therefore to a specific need); they are usually regularly reviewed (rather than being indefinitely available); they are usually flexible enough to respond to short-term use. All these are features of the 'best' resources.

Resource services differ in their availability, flexibility, roles and in the type of resource they offer: human resources, equipment or programs. Services may be formal or informal, widely available, or respond to a purely local need.

Some resource services offer consultancy but even this varies in the type of consultancy offered, its format and whether it is offered to the person with the disability, staff or other community members. A consultancy service might provide assessment and direct intervention, advice about particular tasks, behaviour and programs, or informal consultation about general issues (perhaps 'disability' or 'child development').

Some resource services are a major source of information and ideas for developing suitable individual integration programs, particularly if the individual planning committee decides that additional or alternative program content is needed. The service may have specific ready-made programs: a step-by-step program to teach Jane to type using only her left hand, or a program to teach human relations to a group of young teenagers who have an intellectual disability. Some services have staff who can adapt a community's existing programs; some services provide general information for a community to use in adapting their own programs.

A service may have personnel who come to a community to provide direct instruction to the person with the disability combined with an advice service to staff. Other services provide a diagnostic facility, perhaps linked with recommendations; they may not provide staff to implement those recommendations, relying instead on the community's own staff.

A community may want a resource service that is very practical—providing materials and equipment to use and techniques to try—rather than one only offering advice. Some services specialise in advice about choosing equipment and in training to gain best use from the equipment.

Some resource services offer a variety of approaches, and leave the community to decide on the one that best suits its needs, while others provide one service only.

Some don't provide what they say they will!

Careful consideration enables a community to compare resource services, to choose and use one to best advantage.

Consider the type of service needed. A clearly stated resource need, based on program objectives, allows efficient evaluation of the available resource services.

Learn how each service normally operates. Information about how a service operates can be weighed against a community's resource needs. A community can learn about a service's flexibility and constraints, and decide how best to use the service.

Inform the chosen service how best to service this particular community. Negotiate until a clear working relationship is established. Discuss other resources used, their interaction and co-ordination. Resource staff should provide help to the regular community, not turn the regular community into a special setting by telling it what to do.

Consider all available resource services. Avoid continuing with currently or previously used services just because they are familiar; actively evaluate, compare and choose a service. Don't limit considerations to just formal services, but consider regular community and local services:

- *Special needs services* already exist within the hierarchy of some communities like scouts, schools, youth clubs and camping programs to advise and support the integration of scouts, teenagers, students and campers into their local group.

- *Health professionals* like occupational therapists, speech pathologists, physiotherapists, psychologists, podiatrists or social workers at the local community health centre, hospital or specialist agency may be able to assist with programs, equipment and advice; they may also contribute to staff preparation and education about integration.

- *Regular services* that other community members use may relate to the resource need: a local computer store may have people with specialist knowledge; the local employment agency may suggest a special unit looking at employment of people with a disability; the local childcare course may have students who need practical experience, and this need may match with a preschool's need for extra help.

- Local or specialist *libraries*, toy libraries and equipment libraries can be extremely useful.

- *Diagnostic specific voluntary agencies* like the Down Syndrome Association, The Spina Bifida Association or the Specific Learning Disabilities Association may have information, a library or a parent liaison service and be able to link a community into a wider resource network.

- *Disability specific specialist agencies* like the Spastic Society, the Institute for the Blind or the Deafness Foundation may have units to support integration, provide visiting specialist staff or library resources, be a source of information for staff education, a resource bank of ideas or a channel to find out about other resources.
- *Formal parent support groups or individual parents* may or may not have the answer to a specific query, but they may be part of a resource network that does.
- *Government agencies* may provide a resource service related to either a specific disability or disadvantage (e.g intellectual disability, child abuse or aboriginal children) or a specific skill area (education, employment or housing).
- *Equipment centres* are run by many specialist agencies, including equipment libraries, with staff to advise on the selection of equipment.
- *Staff resource networks* can provide staff with practical ideas and advice from other experienced people.
- *'Disability Resource Centres'* operate in some communities as a central source of information, advice, support, literature, speakers, facts and figures about people with a disability.

PROGRAMS IN OTHER COMMUNITIES

Sometimes resource services act as an information bank of programs available in the wider community. Some programs may be partly or primarily for people who have a disability and thus may not represent integration into a regular community group (they are specialist 'disabled' programs); however they may provide a variety of experiences and thus more chances and choices than would otherwise be available. For some people who have a disability, they may be a step towards a regular community group:

- *Attendant care*—a person with a disability is directly paid a grant to employ an assistant for non-medical tasks that are difficult or time-consuming: personal or household tasks, banking, shopping, transport, mobility, accompaniment to particular events, or assistance with recreational activities.
- *Leisure buddies/leisure partners/cobbers*—a person with a disability is matched with a volunteer to share friendship and new activities.
- *Foster grandparents*—volunteers act as grandparents providing special friendship and outings.
- *Interchange*—a community-based program which matches a child who has a disability with a 'host' family who provides regular occasional care.
- *Camping programs*—in a regular group with an assistant or in a group of campers who all have a disability.

- *Youth groups, guides and scouts* often have established programs to assist the integration of people with a disability into their clubs.

- *Citizen advocacy*—a community-based program which establishes one-to-one relationships between advocates and adults who have a disability. Advocates offer friendship and support, protect the rights and interests of the person with the disability and assist them to speak for themselves.

- *Parent advocacy*—the parents of the person who has the disability choose a person to help them express their point of view and advocate for their child's rights. Some parents find this useful when dealing with community leaders, staff, service providers or an individual planning committee.

- *Self-advocacy* where a person with a disability speaks out for herself and represents her own rights.

RESOURCE CHECKLIST

A review of resources forms part of the review of the individual integration program. The program checklist (p 88) reviews program content and format and this chapter provides a complementary checklist to review program resources; program content, format and resources are intertwined. A resource checklist chart (p 103) can be used for each resource need identified by the individual planning committee to help the committee both choose a resource that complies with the principles of integration and evaluate the effectiveness of the chosen resource.

List the objective and the resource need. A resource should relate to an objective: not 'another pair of hands' but a person 'to help John on the toilet', or 'to interpret instructions into sign language'; not 'a typewriter', but 'a quick, neat way for Jane to write and read back material'; not 'someone to tell me what to do' but 'someone to teach me about program modification'.

Is the resource need community-referenced? Is this resource based on this person's current needs in this community, not on presumed needs or last year's needs?

What is the least restrictive resource type? Would equipment, a human resource or an individual program format be less stigmatising for this person in this environment? High-technology equipment—like a braille-to-print computer—may raise the status of the person who uses it but an adult assistant may lower his status. A calculator may raise status but a childish program may lower it.

What is the least restrictive use of this resource type? Is the equipment, human or program resource used in the least stigmatising way and for the minimum amount of time needed? Does it minimise the involve-ment of special equipment, paid people and formal services? If resources are equally effective, choose regular services before specialist services, an easier technique before equipment, well designed ordinary equipment before 'special' equipment, general assistance before skilled help, a prog-ram relevant for all community members before a 'special' program. Will a visiting teacher produce more stigma than a teacher within the school who is recognised as a 'special needs' teacher? Will a resource person working in the community (the classroom, the job, the pool, the bus) be less stigmatising than a person working at the same skills in a withdrawal program or outside regular hours? Is this equipment appropriate to this person's age and status? A clear cup or glass is more appropriate for an adult than a pink or blue one. A young adult assistant is more appropriate to accompany a teenager to the movies than a middle-aged person.

Identify the resource that meets the resource need in the least restrictive way: 'general assistance to help John when he needs to go to the toilet', 'a human resource skilled in sign language', 'a portable large-print type-writer' or 'skilled assistance with program modification'.

Can existing resources be re-organised? Resource reorganisation should be tried before outside resources are considered. Changes can be made in equipment use, program format (buddy systems or co-operative learning), staff utilisation (team teaching, using existing volunteers) and grouping of community members (mixed ability groups or paired activi-ties).

Are outside resources needed? If re-organisation of existing resources doesn't meet the resource need, additional equipment, additional human resources or a resource service may be needed.

When is this resource needed and used? For what parts of the day or week, and for how long is the resource needed? Is it only available at particular times and do these times match identified needs? Is it available to the staff members who need it most or only to those who ask most often?

Does this resource complement other resources? Are other resources used in the program? Does this resource overlap or contradict other re-sources provided?

Is the resource effective? Does it meet the resource need? Does it let community members perform their roles more confidently and competent-ly? Would lack of this resource take staff away from their role? Does it facilitate the teacher to teach, the swimming coach to coach, the choir conductor to conduct, the bus tour driver to drive? Does the resource leave school as a place for a child to learn and develop, not a place to receive therapy? Does it leave the workplace as a place that produces goods

RESOURCE CHECKLIST

Date...... Client name...................

OBJECTIVE AND RESOURCE NEED	

....
....
....

RESOURCE NEED IS COMMUNITY-REFERENCED	this person	this community	now	
	[ ]	[ ]	[ ]	

RESOURCE TYPE IS LEAST RESTRICTIVE	equipment	human	program	other
	[ ]	[ ]	[ ]	[ ]

RESOURCE USE IS LEAST RESTRICTIVE	commercially available	general assistance	general program	other
	[ ]	[ ]	[ ]	[ ]
	'special' equipment	skilled assistance	specific program	
	[ ]	[ ]	[ ]	

IDENTIFIED RESOURCE	

....
....
....

EXISTING RESOURCES ARE RE-ORGANISED	equipment	human	program format	other
	[ ]	[ ]	[ ]	[ ]

EXTRA RESOURCES ARE NEEDED	equipment	human	services	
	[ ]	[ ]	[ ]	

RESOURCE IS NEEDED days .... time ....

RESOURCE IS USED days .... time ....

RESOURCE COMPLEMENTS OTHERS — other resources used:
a) .... b) .... c) ....

	a)	b)	c)
no overlap	[ ]	[ ]	[ ]
no contradiction	[ ]	[ ]	[ ]

REVIEW DATE ../../....

efficiently, not one that has to take time to teach about canteen routines and punctuality? Does it allow all community members to fully participate and share equally in staff time?

Does this resource have a review date? The 'best' resources are regularly reviewed to maintain their effectiveness.

Resources are tools that can help integration work. Equipment, programs and services can all help integration, but people are the best resource for integration. 'People make integration happen, make integration as natural, right and as effective as it can be' (chapter 3).

Chapter Ten

EFFECTIVE PROCESSES

You can't judge integration by appearances; the observation that a teenager is wearing Op-shop clothes indicates neither that integration is happening nor that it isn't happening. It isn't what she wears but *why* she wears those clothes that is important. It is the *process* which leads the teenager to wear the Op-shop clothes that is the indicator of integration. Similarly the presence of expensive or high-technology resources neither indicates that integration is happening nor that it isn't happening. It isn't the resources themselves but the process of appropriately choosing and using the resources that is the indicator of integration.

Any process can use the principles of integration as a guide to acknowledging rights and allowing risks and choices. Processes which are crucial to the success of integration include decision-making, meeting and problem-solving processes, and processes of choice and risk. Each of these has another process in common—they all depend on good communication.

COMMUNICATION PROCESSES

Good communication is important. The communication that a community uses indicates how that community works. Aimless, irregular, value-laden or rigid communications indicate a disorganised, closed community; specific, directional, purposeful communications are a sign of organisation, of a community's capacity to make integration work. Honest, rational, non-judgemental communication makes integration able to happen and makes it likely to work. If communication is good, then integration benefits from the perspectives, experiences and enthusiasm of community members. Communication has many roles to play in integration:

- Communications reflect attitudes and values which can heavily influence integration's success.
- Media communications can reflect attitudes and values that support integration.
- Communication is the focus of meetings.
- Effective communication is crucial to effective decisions.
- Communication promotes effective problem-solving.

- Communication is the crux of interaction and interdependence between community members.

Good communication can be difficult.   Good communication is vital for integration, but it can be difficult to achieve because of the sheer numbers of people involved. An individual planning committee may be attended by a couple of people or by a large group; 50 people may have direct contact with the person who has the disability (the staff and classmates at a school); the community may have hundreds of people (including other students and their parents). To be effective, communication for integration sometimes requires different information and different communication formats, each matched to particular people. Information that is suitable for individual planning committee members may not be suitable for the hundreds of people participating in the community itself.

Communication can be hampered by differences in both people's goals for integration and the processes they support to reach that goal. Unless they communicate these differences to each other, different people may try to help the integration of the same person into the same community but be working towards different goals and providing help in different ways. This confusion makes integration less effective than it can be.

Good communication can also be difficult because the processes that make integration most effective also make communication more complicated. Linking with programs in other communities, using resource services and individualising programs can certainly all make integration more effective; however they all complicate communication by involving people with different perspectives, experiences and knowledge. Additionally it is not just information that is needed from these people; integration requires sharing ideas, attending meetings, reaching decisions and problem-solving with them. These all involve complex communications.

Good communication can be learned.   People can develop the skill of communicating effectively and, what's more, learn to communicate to their advantage. Books and courses are available for developing better communication skills in specific situations that can be useful for integration—negotiating, running meetings, effective parenting, public speaking and writing reports.

Good communication is specific.   Specific communication avoids misinterpretations and disappointment.

> *A parent*:   I don't ask 'Is it accessible?' any more but I ask more specific things like 'Are there any steps?', 'Is the toilet wide enough for a wheelchair?'

Each communication has a purpose and a direction.   Good communication has a purpose—to pass on *specific information* to a *specific person* for a *specific purpose*. It also has a direction, perhaps a number of directions; it is not aimless. Knowing each communication's purpose and direction helps clarify how to make it most effective.

- *Specific information* indicates the important parts of the communication.

- To a *specific person* indicates both the information that is relevant for that person and an appropriate language level.

- For a *specific purpose* indicates an appropriate communication format. Would verbal or written information be more suitable? Would a diagram be easiest or a video (or a song, a book or film!)?

Identifying communication's purpose and direction also helps stop breaches of confidentiality. Good communication doesn't use or pass on information just because it is available.

Good communication is assertive. 'Being assertive means being aware of your own rights, and expressing your thoughts and feelings in direct, honest ways that do not ignore the rights of other people. The goals of assertion are giving and getting respect, asking for fair play and leaving room for compromise.... Because assertion leaves room for compromise and for different people's viewpoints, it can stop a person feeling swayed by the offers, efforts and feelings of other people, even those of "do-gooders"' (chapter 15). A simple assertive statement can lessen strained feelings, tense meetings and bitter arguments and can give people what they want from communications—comfortable, useful interactions that achieve their purpose.

Communication should reflect the principles of integration. Good communication doesn't use questions, statements or decisions based on presumptions about other people's attitudes, knowledge or skills. It doesn't make presumptions of categorisation ('All blind people have wonderfully sensitive hands') or of segregation ('They're happier with their own kind'); it reflects social justice and equal opportunity.

Good communication states the unstated. Good communication relies on observable information and clearly stated facts. Just as it doesn't make presumptions, good communication doesn't rely on people presuming or implying anything from the communication. Good communication doesn't leave things to interpretation or misinterpretation, to clarification or expansion. It states the unstated.

Stating the unstated helps clarify objectives. 'Students are to work independently at desks' is an unstated presumption at secondary school. By stating it, its importance for integration becomes obvious and, likewise, its importance as an objective becomes obvious.

Good communication involves active listening. Communication is a two way process; it is not just the giving of information but involves actively receiving information. Good communication requires paying attention and following the ideas in the communication, and not interrupting or diverting the communicator. It involves attending to what the communicator is really saying and not jumping to early conclusions. Active listening promotes an understanding of other people's perspectives.

A communication book can be useful. In many integration situations a 'communication book' ensures accurate, up-to-date communication. It can provide a link between communities, particularly if the person has trouble communicating pertinent information. It could include written comments by staff and a memento or sample of the person's activities: a leaf from a walk, a sample of his cooking or a photo of the cricket team. Good and bad, happy and sad, liked and disliked events can all be included. Which ones were the most important from this person's perspective?

A communication book should not be used unconfidentially to report incidents which the person would not have reported if she could communicate better. (Would a child normally tell her parents if she'd taken a friend's lollies?)

Another type of communication book can be designed to share programming/performance information and be used as a record. This type of book can be particularly useful for consultants who don't often have contact with the person who has the disability. They can then efficiently see information chronologically covering all the communities in which the person is involved.

MEETING PROCEDURES

Effective integration usually requires meetings, many meetings, effective meetings. To be effective, like any form of communication, meetings need a purpose, need to avoid presumptions and to respect confidentiality. A meeting's purpose is often to make decisions, particularly if it is a committee meeting like an individual planning committee meeting. However the process of 'surviving meetings' is separate from 'decision-making'.

SURVIVING MEETINGS

People who attend meetings often have vastly different experience in attending, contributing to and using meetings. Some people may frequently attend meetings and be skilled at running meetings in an equitable way. Other people may frequently attend meetings and be quite skilled at using meetings for their own purpose! Other people may be attending their first meeting.

Formal meeting procedures can provide a firm footing and encourage purposeful, specific communications—effective for integration. Some meetings about integration are run according to strict meeting procedures, however following strict meeting procedures is not always in the best interests of integration. Meetings designed to help integration work aim to share information which is then used to make decisions. Adherence to strict meeting procedures may intimidate some people from sharing the information that they have, particularly if they are unfamiliar with meetings, let alone meeting procedures.

Whatever the meeting format, some factors can help all committee members survive meetings, perhaps help them contribute to meetings, hopefully help them use meetings and maybe even help them enjoy (yes, enjoy!) meetings.

Meetings need a purpose and an agenda. Like all forms of communication, meetings need a specific purpose. Having a meeting just because 'We scheduled one for today' or 'The regulations state that we must have a meeting' is not a specific purpose. Meetings can be called for the wrong purpose—unnecessarily or out of habit—or be re-scheduled as a way of avoiding decisions.

Effective meetings have an overall purpose that is the same each time the committee meets (perhaps to help integration be successful) and a new agenda for each meeting. The agenda, a list of the issues to be discussed, changes for each meeting according to the current issues.

The overall purpose of the committee or the specific items on the agenda usually determines who attends. There is no perfect number of people for a perfect meeting (if only there were!)—an individual planning committee may be attended by a couple of people or by a large group (chapter 8).

The agenda is known to all committee members. Effective meetings inform all committee members about the agenda before they attend the meeting. New or temporary committee members can be listed too, and then members can better consider what they want to say and be prepared to be specific and purposeful: if the work experience employer will attend the meeting, the agenda can include items about work preparation and vocational planning; if staff from the community residence will be attending, a committee member may want to add 'increasing independence in personal hygiene' to the agenda.

Sometimes the agenda is not obvious. A mother may spontaneously go to see the school principal, who then may not know the agenda until she tells him. If she has a clear agenda for discussion (in her mind or on paper) she can be effective in telling the principal of the agenda and in sticking to it.

Regular meetings can be useful. Regular meetings are responsible and effective if they are used not just for crisis management but to share good news, progress and achievements. No wonder people dislike meetings if they always indicate bad news, discouragement and the hard work that will follow. Regular meetings are useful if their frequency reflects their purpose. They can be an ongoing source of ideas, can form part of a support network (chapter 9) and can indicate a long-term commitment by the community to integration's success. Regular meetings continually reinforce the notion of sharing, that integration is something to which all people contribute; it is not the result of one person's hard work or of luck.

The location and format of a meeting may influence its effectiveness. A meeting's location and format can affect its outcome because the person who it most familiar with the location has an advantage. A principal holding the meeting at school is on home ground, but other people may feel less at ease and find it difficult to be natural; they may have memories of unsuccessful schooldays. Holding a meeting at the home of the person who has the disability may be intrusive and reinforce his feeling of being public property (chapter 4). It may add pressure to him to not only survive the meeting but also to be a host. At a formal table people may take a meeting more seriously. If food and drink are consumed throughout, people often see the actual meeting content as incidental and/or insignificant.

Meeting records are important.   Effective meetings have shared written agendas and keep minutes—a written record of the meeting. The minutes list meeting participants, and itemise the agenda, the main points of discussion and any decisions that follow. A useful addition to minutes is an 'action column' indicating the committee member who will be responsible for acting on that item. (This is a good basis for setting the agenda for the next meeting, too). Minutes should be available to committee members promptly after the meeting so that they can carry out the responsibilities allotted to them in the action column, and report back on them at the next meeting.

Consider keeping personal records.   Some people keep personal records or a diary of formal and informal meetings, including agendas, minutes, phone conversations and a list of any jargon or abbreviations and their meanings. This can be useful when attending different meetings about integration for the one person—to accurately relay information and assist co-ordination.

Some people record items for their own agenda. While a meeting is in progress they write down items to bring up later rather than interrupt the meeting or risk forgetting the items.

Know the committee members.   If someone is unfamiliar with other committee members or their roles they can ask for further information. They should be dissatisfied with role titles if it isn't clear what that title means. Other people can explain how well they know the person with the disability, for how long they've known her, how recently they've seen her and what 'parts' of her they know. Such explanations help committee members learn the jargon that surrounds integration.

Know yourself.   If a person knows himself well he can better prepare for meetings—he can choose and use personal strategies to keep things going smoothly. He may find that role play or self-talk (chapter 16) helps him prepare and manage meetings. He may feel confident using humour (chapter 14) to put people at ease, to avoid an outburst of anger and to manage potentially uncomfortable situations.

If a person knows her own thresholds (chapter 12) she can more comfortably decide on items for the agenda—when to bring up big issues or which issues she's prepared to let pass. She may be able to avoid difficult situations and a sense of obligation.

By taking the initiative (chapter 13) a person can avoid potentially difficult situations and establish common ground in meetings. He can acknowledge other people's perspectives and opinions while still stressing similarities.

Get some help. Some people find that using an advocate (chapter 9) helps them gain confidence and support in meetings and have their point of view clearly represented.

DECISION-MAKING PROCESSES

Integration requires effective decisions which are best made at effective meetings. The variety of services used in integration, the number of people involved and their different perspectives can complicate decision-making just as much as they can complicate communication.

Decision-making can be particularly difficult in integration because the decision to be made is often between many different points of view, not just between two points of view. Because of integration's nature (chances and choices for everyone) many different factors and perspectives have to be considered. People sometimes jump to the conclusion that a particular decision unfairly favours one person's perspective over another. However, just as integration can't be judged by appearances, a decision-making process shouldn't be judged by the decision it makes; unpopular decisions may result from good decision-making processes. It's the process behind the decision that's important.

PROMOTING EFFECTIVE DECISION-MAKING

Decisions are made in different ways, and people can influence this process to encourage an effective decision-making process—one that considers the opinions of, and allows discussion between, all the decision-makers (voters) until a decision acceptable to them all is reached.

Good communication is essential for effective decision-making.
Communication is difficult in integration because of the number of people involved and their different perspectives, but it is even more difficult for the same number of people to make a group decision. They are certainly not going to make an effective decision unless they have good communication processes. If a decision will be based on the communication, good communication is even more important—be specific, avoid presumptions, state the unstated, actively listen and be confidential.

Assertive communications encourage effective decision-making.
Assertive communication (chapter 15) avoids a 'right or wrong' approach and promotes direct, honest expression of thoughts and feelings while

considering the rights of other people. This is vital to good decision-making because it avoids confrontation, where each person (or group of people) communicates their perspective without acknowledging the existence of other perspectives, let alone the right of other people to have a different perspective. Through being assertive, people can indicate their understanding of other people's opinions and their acceptance that their own opinion will not override or be overrun by other people's opinions, but will be equally weighed.

When committee members communicate assertively, their opinions are more likely to be clearly heard and considered. Committees are only as good as the contributions made to them and the process they use to reach decisions, so it is important that all members of the individual planning committee have the opportunity to express their feelings and to have their opinions heard. Decisions are easiest when communications indicate that each member is cared for, valued, part of a network of communication and obligation, and of support. Assertive communication can help people feel supported in this way.

Effective meeting procedures are essential for effective decision-making.   Meeting records are vital, including accurate minutes of decisions; reaching decisions can be difficult enough without disagreement later about the nature of the actual decision.

TYPES OF DECISION-MAKING

Decisions about integration often involve finding common ground among people of different backgrounds and training, and with different relationships to the decision area (the person with the disability). A decision-making format that accommodates these factors is needed.

Consider consensus and majority-rule decisions.   A *consensus deci-sion* is one that is agreed to by all voters; there is no 'winning' or 'losing' decision, and responsibility for the decision is shared by all the voters. A *majority-rule decision* is one that receives the most votes. Sometimes people who support the 'winning' decision feel that they 'own' the decision, and the people who support the 'losing' option may feel they lost control of the decision and thus have no responsibility for it.

Consider collaborative and consultative decision-making.   'Collaboration gives people most affected by a decision the right to actually share in making that decision.'[10] Collaborative decision-making values each voter's unique skills, and relies on the voters to share information, make a decision by consensus and share responsibility for it.

Consultative decision-making uses advice from non-voting consultants. It assumes there are experts who (because of their experience and training) can provide advice to decision-makers. The consultants do not vote and therefore have no responsibility for the decision or for its implementation. Consultation does not imply commitment to the end decision. An additional difficulty with consultative decision-making is that consultants only pass on to the committee information they thought was relevant or which the committee requested. Because they are not part of a collaborative process, consultants have no responsibility for the decision and so may not share all information that could be useful.

If people with particular expertise become part of a collaborative decision-making process then they will be equally responsible with other voters for sharing information and for the consensus decision reached. Overall, *collaborative decision-making that reaches consensus decisions* works best for integration, for a number of reasons.

- Collaborative decision-making encourages shared information, shared decisions, shared action and shared responsibility.
- Collaboration and consensus best uses the variety of skills and information that various people bring to integration.
- People involved in making decisions are more likely to support those decisions than if they are only told of decisions by the 'decision-makers' and then expected to implement them.

Negotiation promotes effective decision-making. Negotiation is a skill that facilitates collaboration and consensus; it is particularly useful in situations where opinions are not only diverse but appear incompatible. Negotiation aims for mutual benefit through consensus—through a solution that satisfies both people equally. This may involve thinking of a third alternative (different to both the alternatives of the original confrontation), but this third alternative is both an equal compromise and of equal benefit to both people.

A good negotiator gets what she wants but also helps the other person to get what he wants. Negotiation is based on the belief that if both sides don't have some of their needs met, decisions will be poorly implemented if at all. The basis of negotiation is to avoid ultimatums and careless threats, to leave room for the third alternative and for compromise, to stick to the issues, to ask for time if necessary and to not give up. Third, fourth and fifth alternatives should be suggested until a mutual compromise is reached.

PROBLEM-SOLVING PROCESSES

Some individual planning committees are persistent in reviewing and modifying individual integration programs—they are a never-ending source of ideas. Other committees have trouble developing alternative ways to reach their objectives, to solve problems as they arise. Successful problem-solving relies to some extent on the persistency and expertise of committee members, but specific strategies are useful, too.

Lateral thinking helps solve some problems. When faced with a problem it is often easier to recall a familiar solution than to think of new ways and new ideas; unfortunately old ideas do not always solve new problems. *Lateral thinking* involves looking at a situation afresh and reducing the problem to its basic elements. Sometimes it helps to imagine you're a person from Mars seeing the problem for the first time in order to avoid preconceived ideas and the influence of other people's previous solutions.

A parent: I read about a man who had Down syndrome and wanted to join the Army in 1939 like all his mates. His parents suggested he join the Salvation Army and he got his 'uniform' which he wore proudly. He was de-mobbed out of 'uniform' like his mates in 1945.

A parent: John had a variety of ways of getting home from school and a variety of places he went to—speech therapy, Family Day Care, home by bus, car or walking. It was getting confusing. I then started a system of 'tickets' in his bag which told him what he was to do that afternoon. I put the right one in his bag in the morning, he read it in the afternoon and then did the right thing—mostly, anyway!

A teacher: John kept getting his shirt wet using the taps at school for a drink. I showed him how the ground sloped and therefore which tap was the easiest to reach.

A parent: The headmaster told me that they were worried that John kept climbing the trees at school. He wanted to know if we had any ideas about what to do. I asked him what they did when other kids climbed trees. 'We tell them not to' he said. 'Tell John not to' I suggested!

Task analysis helps solve some problems.   'The best of Special Education is not in its buildings or its low-ratio classes or its specially trained teachers—it's in the fundamental principle of Task Analysis.'[10] Task analysis is the step-by-step teaching of a specific skill. A task analysis of 'putting the toothpaste on the brush' includes the steps of locating the toothbrush, locating the toothpaste, removing the toothpaste cap, holding the brush by the handle, holding the toothpaste tube correctly, directing the tube to the bristles of the brush, squeezing an appropriate amount of paste and replacing the cap on the tube. Each step is usually matched to a range of techniques and equipment options.

Task analysis is a problem-solving process that is as relevant to abstract skills like 'punctuality', 'politeness', 'learning to share' or 'learning to conform' as to concrete skills like 'learning to type', 'blowing your nose', 'washing the dishes' or 'using public transport'. It's a simple principle that doesn't need a 'special' environment, special services or special teachers.

RISK AND CHOICE PROCESSES

Effective programs need processes behind them that support the four principles of integration: social justice, equal opportunity, non-categorisation and non-segregation. Application of these principles to decisions about program content and format sometimes leads to dilemmas about self-determination versus protection, and conservative versus unusual choices.

Simple solutions are best

SELF-DETERMINATION VERSUS PROTECTION

The principles of integration support the notion of self-determination, that a person should be able to make choices about her life. However, self-determination is not the same as a licence to do what you want, as a limitless allowance; self-determination indicates a measure of constraint. Self-determination implies the ability to self-deny, to postpone pleasure, to use judgement and apply some balance.

The greatest difficulty for some people in acknowledging a person's right to self-determination is in the area of risk-taking. They believe that people with a disability don't have enough experience to make decisions and are less able to weigh the advantages and disadvantages of a situation, and to use balance and control to make rational choices. They feel that people with a disability will be vulnerable to accidents, abuse and financial exploitation, and thus need some protection.

The idea of 'protection' is like the consultative model of decision-making, where some people 'know best' because of their experience and training. Protection is a difficult idea to match with integration because integration acknowledges people's rights and choices. Integration offers choices knowing that some of those choices will be risky but also knowing that people learn by taking risks. In contrast, protection assumes that a decision made by a person of a higher intellect or ability (a 'protector's' decision) leads to a better choice. This is a major assumption—it is particularly difficult to make decisions for a person who has different abilities and experiences to oneself, as is usually the case with a person who has a disability and the person making decisions about protection.

Some people see dangers in protection, believing that it leads to frustration, loss of dignity and of self-esteem. They believe protection blocks the principles of integration and leads to reduced opportunities and increased categorisation and segregation. Additionally they believe that a person who is used to a high degree of protection is vulnerable when that protection is reduced by even a small amount.

A solution that is compatible with the principles of integration, and still allows for varying abilities and experiences, is to use self-determination as a starting point and work back towards protection rather than use protection as a starting point and work towards self-determination. This applies the principle of the least restrictive alternative (chapter 3) to self-determination. It results in the least protection, most self-determination, most choices and reasonable risks.

CONSERVATIVE VERSUS UNUSUAL CHOICES

Attitudes towards integration will be most positive when people with a disability are seen as ordinary people, doing ordinary things and making 'ordinary' choices. Some people find other people's opinions irrelevant; they make a choice knowing that people may disapprove of their choice or make presumptions about them. Choice is vital for integration, but real choice implies knowledge not only of the range of choices, but also the ways that the choice may be interpreted by other people.

A middle-of-the-road course sometimes makes integration more successful. It helps avoid the chance of 'different' behaviour being seen as related to a person's disability rather than to his choice to be different.

- 'A blind person may wear loud coloured clothes not because 'She's blind and doesn't know how to match her wardrobe, poor thing'. She may choose to be a flamboyant dresser.
- A person in a wheelchair may have an untidy house not because 'He can't do it all, you know'. He may just not choose to value a tidy house.' (chapter 3)

Chapter 11 suggests choosing 'activities that don't encourage common negative stereotypes of people who have a disability. Offer a choice of activities that promotes a positive image—at the park encourage an adult to feed the ducks or play cricket rather than play in the sandpit. If she enjoys sand, let her do so at the beach where other adults also enjoy sand.' By discouraging an adult from playing in the sandpit her choices are reduced, and it could be argued that this is against the philosophy of integration where choice is vital. Choice *is* vital, but real choice requires knowledge and experience of the available choices and their outcomes. Introducing a variety of activities at the park may provide more choices than this person had considered.

Positive attitudes towards integration need not be overt; they can still be below community consciousness.

> Conservative and even old fashioned lifestyles are more likely to be respected or ignored by the general public than avante garde and experimental ones. People with handicaps are already in the forefront of one social movement. They can't afford to be used as (examples of other social change movements).[11]

A middle-of-the-road course can help keep integration below community consciousness; integration is then as ordinary as it can be—something that happens rather than something to remark upon.

Integration is a process, not a static situation. Successful integration uses other processes in order to remain successful, to provide maximum choices and minimum risks.

Chapter Eleven

INTERACTION AND INTERDEPENDENCE BETWEEN COMMUNITY MEMBERS

'Integration means not just being together but doing activities together. It is not just polite attendance at a community or participation in its activities; it also implies interaction and interdependence between community members. Integration means being part of a community, belonging to the community' (chapter 3).

Interdependence is an important aspect of 'being part of a community' and of friendship between community members. Friendship is not one-sided; friendship involves interdependence—friends give and take, friends help each other. Friendship can be important to a person who has a disability. Some people with a disability are involved in few communities because of lack of resources and inappropriate programs. Those communities with which they are involved may overlap (perhaps a sheltered workshop community that provides work and social activities with the same people) and so offer a limited choice of friendships. Few people may take the time to get to know a person who has a disability and so their choice of friends may be further limited.

Additionally, people who have a disability often have many 'professionals' surrounding them: doctors, therapists, teachers, assistants. 'Hovering' professionals or adults can limit a person's opportunities to interact spontaneously with other people, to try out new relationships and 'test' friendships in normal ways.

No-one is accepted and admired by everyone because people accept and admire different things. However everyone needs acceptance by someone, and the more people who know a person with a disability (which is more likely through interaction), the more likely he is to be accepted and to be integrated into the lives of that group of people.

Integration is usually considered successful when a person with a disability is an equal part of a community, enjoying the good aspects and suffering the difficult aspects of that community along with other community members. Integration is often considered most successful when it is low-key, when a person's disability is below the community's consciousness, when she is simply getting on with her life as a community member (chapter 17). It is the interactions of that person with other community members that leads to the integration of her choices and abilities into the community's wide range of lifestyles, choices and abilities, when she is accepted as a community member.

118

Being there: attendance doesn't guarantee interaction

'Acceptance' may not be simply the opposite of 'rejection'. Just because a person *doesn't* reject something doesn't mean he accepts it. He may not reject cold brussel sprouts, blood sports or people who have a disability, but that doesn't mean that he involves himself with them, chooses them, accepts them, tolerates them or likes them. It simply means that he doesn't reject them. So stopping rejection of something doesn't mean it has been accepted. Stopping rejection of people with a disability doesn't mean that they have been accepted.

Contact with people who have a disability will not on its own lead to acceptance of them but the right sorts of contacts will certainly assist such acceptance. Community members learn something about people who have a disability when they see facilities for them in the community. They learn more when they actually see people who have a disability using ordinary community facilities and doing ordinary things like shopping, crossing the road and using a telephone. They learn even more when people with a disability do 'clever' things like working or going to school; 'fun' things like dancing, playing football or putting a bet on the races; 'exotic' things like running a marathon, making a lot of money or travelling overseas. However, community members learn most when they actually shop, cross the road, go to school, work or play football with people who have a disability—when they interact and are interdependent with them.

Such real-life interdependence with people who have a disability is more important in the development of a positive attitude towards integration than 'education' about disability. 'Disability awareness activities' (chapter 7) have their place but ongoing appropriate interaction and interdependence with people who have a disability is more effective.

Everyday contact and interdependence between community members helps them develop low-key, accepting attitudes. Positive attitudes towards integration need not be overt; they can be ordinary attitudes, not strongly positive, not consciously thought about. Integration can just become part of the fabric of everyday life.

IDEAS TO ENCOURAGE INTERACTION AND INTERDEPENDENCE

Interaction between people presumes that these people have something in common (or enough in common to interact with each other), that they recognise this and that they also have the social skills to communicate this 'commonness'. It presumes that these people want to interact, can interact and know what they want to interact about.

Integration may be a new experience, both for people with a disability and for people without a disability, and some of these people may not want to know each other (chapter 4). Even if they do want to interact, they may not know how to do so. Their interaction and interdependence can be encouraged by the use of particular program formats and by the example of staff attitudes. Both these factors will help community members form opinions and attitudes based on fact not on fears, based on individuals not categories—based on reality.

ATTITUDES

Staff have a responsibility to not only implement the individual integration program (chapter 8), but to implement it in a way that encourages interaction and interdependence between all community members—in a way that shows the ordinariness of people with a disability.

Set a good example. Integration works when people's attitudes let it happen. It doesn't depend on particular laws, facilities, programs or people, though they can each play their part. The behaviour, conversations, decisions and interaction of community members can all show attitudes that understand integration, that reflect social justice—that allow a person with a disability the right to participate, to learn, to disagree, to conform, to take responsibility, to be individual, to make mistakes and to try again. (Each of these attitudes is expanded in chapter 3.)

- An attitude of non-categorisation.
- An attitude of non-segregation.
- An attitude recognising people's rights.
- An attitude of acceptance of people's individuality.
- An attitude of respect for disability.
- An attitude that allows people to take responsibility for their decisions.

Modelling of co-operative, caring behaviour has more impact on members' attitudes than 'teaching' them about such behaviour. Staff can indicate, through example, that community members have an obligation to consider all the other members of the community.

Provide community education. Staff can show appropriate ways to interact with, help and encourage a particular person who has a disability without holding a formal 'demonstration of how to do it' (chapter 7).

They can use ordinary words rather than words that underline differences: 'play with pets' rather than 'pet therapy', 'enjoys water' rather than 'hydrotherapy'.

PROGRAMS

Although the individual integration program identifies needed aspects of the program content and format, staff often have the opportunity to use informal or social activities to further develop the sense of belonging of all community members.

Choose activities carefully.   An activity is the medium that provides the focus for interest and interaction. Staff can take the initiative (chapter 13) and choose an activity that provides common ground between community members and emphasises their similarities. If, from time to time, the community chooses an activity at which a person with a disability is skilled, this allows her to impress the group, particularly if the activity is currently popular and therefore highly valued.

> *A parent*:   It is lovely being the parent of the child who wins the sack race even if it is because his legs are so short that he doesn't have to shorten his stride.

Activities should be based on what people *can* do, rather than *ought* to be able to do. Activities that allow people to contribute at their own level are particularly useful. Any rules or constraints on the activity should be kept to a minimum and not rely on complicated verbal descriptions, but use a variety of instruction and communication formats.

Try activities that involve everyone and where everyone is a winner (co-operative activities rather than competitive activities). Avoid activities where people have to wait for a turn or are forced 'out' (unless learning to tolerate such a social situation is an objective that the individual planning committee has identified).

Choose activities that don't encourage common negative stereotypes of people with a disability. Offer a choice of activities that promotes a positive image—at the park encourage an adult to feed the ducks or play cricket rather than play in the sandpit. If she enjoys sand, let her do so at the beach where other adults enjoy sand.

Paired activities can encourage interdependence.   Paired activities certainly require one-to-one interaction but can also be used to develop interdependence if each person in the pair has a turn to be the leader/the demonstrator/the one who chooses the activity and then has a turn being the follower.

Peer tutoring, learning and teaching shared between community members, can give a person with a disability the opportunity to 'give' as well as 'take' and to demonstrate competence and skill in the eyes of other community members and staff.

> *A parent*: My son does a wonderful song and dance act to 'Born in the U.S.A.' He does an incredibly accurate take-off of Bruce Springsteen including taking his shirt off and swinging it around. He knows he's good at it, and his self-esteem soars when he's had a chance to show the other kids how to do this.

'Peer tutoring is a valuable component of any integration program. It is relatively easy to set up and can become a focus area for building acceptance, understanding and friendship between disabled and non-disabled students.'[12]

Cross-age tutoring, learning and teaching shared between community members of different ages, also encourages interdependence. It allows practice of basic skills or concepts without loss of self-esteem—friends are helping rather than the 'teacher' teaching. A person with a disability may benefit from being either the younger or older part of the cross-age pair: 'Senior students derive much satisfaction from tutoring younger students and the youngsters achieve maturity earlier.'[9] Cross-age tutoring may meet a particular social development objective.

Co-operative activities encourage interaction.

'The structuring of co-operative learning experiences promotes a process of acceptance.'[13] Working *with* other people for a common goal creates more understanding than working *alongside* them towards similar but separate goals.

Additionally co-operative activities encourage sharing the responsibility and the pleasure of achievement. Acceptance and use of individual skills and interests is encouraged because each person only achieves if the group as a whole achieves. Such co-operative activity among mixed ability groups encourages group spirit because the program 'revolves around co-operative effort, centred on activity, rather than a more competitive process in a lock-step system, where the product is a mark rather than the satisfaction of achieving a task.'[9]

With co-operative activities there is a risk that some people may contribute less to the activity than others, but an experienced staff member can guard against this by providing more structure—perhaps choosing a non-competitive task and carefully dividing the task's work among group members.

Offer flexibility...

The provision of a range of activities that caters for a variety of skills, interests and abilities reduces the air of competitiveness present when all group members are performing their own version of the same activity. 'Competitive and individualistic learning experiences tend to promote a process of rejection within which non-disabled students' negative impressions of disabled peers are continued and increased.'[13] The activities should be matched with materials, equipment and resources which cater for various interest and ability levels. Various communication and instruction formats should be available and a variation in quality and quantity of outputs should be accepted.

Increased staff interactions with a person who has a disability may reduce that person's interaction with other people—'Retarded children who get more teacher initiated interactions get less social exchange with their peer group.'[8] Use resources in the least restrictive way, which may vary from activity to activity.

...*but provide enough structure.* People learn about interacting with each other if activities are chosen so that the same people meet a number of times. This is much better than a token 'social visit' (chapter 8), an introduction that has little chance to grow into understanding or friendship.

Provide enough structure by taking the initiative (chapter 13) to acknowledge differences and avoid problems. Use problem-solving strategies (chapter 10) and appropriate resources (chapter 9) to increase a person's attendance and participation in the activity, and his interaction and interdependence with community members.

Program content can encourage understanding, interaction and interdependence. *Disability awareness activities* (chapter 7) can encourage general understanding and knowledge about disability, but they don't provide specific information about individual people.

A person with a disability can often benefit from belonging to a small, easily identifiable group, and may most easily gain and give support—be interdependent—in this sort of environment. *Peer support programs*— which use a senior community member to assist junior members in learning the social aspects of the community—can offer this type of group. With support from older members, younger ones can gain self-awareness and the ability to resist harmful peer pressures. Older members provide a safe environment to share feelings in a non-judgemental atmosphere, and have the chance to develop leadership skills through structured activities in the peer support program.

Programs to develop *self-esteem* in community members can often give them the confidence to interact. Measures of children's overall self-esteem are only weakly connected to their popularity and academic achievement. But children's perceptions of their abilities in particular areas (e.g. football or reading) are closely connected to their actual ability in that area. So, although children know their abilities (and thus presumably their disabilities), their knowledge may not affect their self-esteem. However many factors *do* affect their self-esteem (regardless of their abilities and disabilities), and particular strategies can be used to give every community member the opportunity to build their self-esteem: listen to and acknowledge the thoughts and feelings of all community members; structure situations to help them experience feelings of success; give them a reasonable sense of control over their lives (choices and responsibilities); reinforce them as capable and lovable; model a positive view of yourself and use words that express encouragement, not just exaggerated praise.

The existence of 'integration programs' and 'integration resources' will not, on their own, make integration happen. Resources and programs can encourage community attendance and program participation, but it is community members' interaction and interdependence that makes integration work.

PART FOUR: **KEEP GOING!**

Part four reinforces the idea that integration is an ongoing process. Integration is not a static state but is a process that changes to meet the needs of different people, that changes over time, through circumstances and across communities. More importantly, integration is a process that can be changed through attitudes and efforts.

Successful integration involves interaction—not only discussion, planning and meetings between many people from various backgrounds, but interaction between people who have a disability and those who don't. People have different ideas, hopes and concerns about integration, yet respect between them is vital for integration to work. Strong personal and interactional skills help people express ideas, understand other people's viewpoints and reach agreement despite varying attitudes, skills and levels of commitment. Personal and interactional skills can thus help people with varying attitudes to successfully work together.

Part four also describes how to guide and support integration—how to evaluate integration processes and programs and to address problems that arise. Part four describes how to keep the process of integration progressing towards equal chances and choices for everyone.

Chapter Twelve

KNOW YOUR OWN THRESHOLDS

Just as people have thresholds for physical pain they also have thresholds for emotional feelings. People can use knowledge about emotional thresholds to become more comfortable and effective in all sorts of integration situations.

Knowing your own thresholds is a weighing up process balancing the advantages of a particular situation or course of action against its disadvantages, then assessing the importance of the outcome while taking account of other demands on time and energy. By weighing up a particular situation at a particular time, a person can make a decision based on her current threshold, and minimise the influence of past decisions, other people's expectations and other people's choices. By making a decision about what she wants to say or do in a particular situation, a person can feel more confident and effective in interactions with other people. She can actually make a decision—to ignore the situation or not, to speak out or not comment, to arrange a meeting or write a letter or make a phonecall, to make a statement or ask a question or express an opinion. The alternative might be to drift with circumstances because of lack of a decision. By knowing her thresholds, a person can feel more in control, more positive, more rational and less overloaded.

In integration, many situations require the expressing of opinions, viewpoints, hopes and concerns. People sometimes feel that they don't manage these situations as well as they have at other times or as well as they would like. This may be because people's thresholds vary for different situations, for different types of comments or for expressing comments with different people. Knowing your own thresholds gives people the confidence to judge each situation in relation to themselves (not other people), in relation to today (not last time) and in relation to the particular issue.

Knowing your own thresholds helps with surviving meetings. Recognising thresholds helps a person decide on agenda items: whether to bring up big issues, when to wait for another time or which issues to let pass this time. It may help a person recognise his need for help in managing meetings, and recognise which type of meeting format is easiest for him. It can lead to recognition of areas where being more assertive could help (chapter 15).

Knowing your own thresholds helps in decision-making. By
weighing up the advantages and disadvantages of a particular decision, a
person may feel that she has *made* a decision rather than let it be made by
other people for her or without her. She has contributed to it—at least in
her own mind—and must therefore take some responsibility for it.

> *A parent*: We need a weekend without Jane every 5 or 6 weeks. Having
> realised this, I have worked towards achieving it—camps, respite care etc.
> Since then I have felt more in control and purposeful.

Knowing your own thresholds helps in choosing a community.

> *A parent*: I was scared of all that could go wrong but I knew nothing
> could be worse than last year's experience at a segregated school.

By evaluating the additional time and effort he is prepared to put into a
community, a person may be more able to choose a community that
matches this. It may also help him evaluate his ability to manage travel to a
more distant community.

Knowing your own thresholds helps in setting limits. By knowing
his thresholds a person can define the type of effort he is prepared to make
(canteen duty but not excursion duty) or the amount of time (number of
days per week on canteen duty). It helps a person avoid a sense of
obligation based on past decisions, past habits or other people's preferences; a person makes a decision based on his thresholds today.

- 'I know you feel more comfortable when we go to the epilepsy
  meetings together, Paul, but I don't feel like going tonight.'
- 'I can help either Thursday mornings or Tuesday afternoons, but not
  both times.'

***Knowing your own thresholds helps avoid setting yourself up in
difficult situations.***

> *A parent*: I found that I was hearing all sorts of things about Jane that
> other parents didn't hear about their kids—when she'd missed the bus or
> was late for line-up. I used to put up with it but recently I decided that I
> didn't want to hear more than I would have if she didn't have a disability
> and I told the staff so.

> *A staff member*: I always talk to both of John's parents together now,
> because I found I couldn't manage the disjointed communications we had
> if I saw them individually.

> *A parent*: We were going to call him Simon 'til we found out he was
> retarded. 'Simple Simon' was more than I could manage so we changed
> his name.

***Knowing your own thresholds helps avoid repeating the same dif-
ficulty.***

> *A parent*: I always felt lousy when the Child Disability Allowance review
> form came; it made me realise how things were. Last time I didn't fill it in,

but wrote across it 'If he improves or a cure for Down syndrome is found, rest assured that you will be among the first people I will inform'. It didn't make any difference to them but I sure felt better.

Knowing your own thresholds helps with recognition of what you want. It is easier to work towards identified goals.

A teacher: I want other teachers to understand my position. I want other teachers to share the responsibility. Okay I'm his teacher, but he's our responsibility as a school.

Knowing your own thresholds helps with recognition of changed thresholds.

A parent: I used to wake up in the morning and think 'What will go wrong today?' Now I think 'I wonder what I can do about so and so.'

A parent: I've got tired of other people thinking John's friends are 'good' or 'kind' when they play with him. I used to put up with it but now I'm mostly confident enough to tell other people that John's friends have their arguments with him just like all friends.

Knowing your own thresholds helps in matching responses to specific situations.

A parent: The word I use depends on how I feel at the time. If I'm not feeling very courageous I'll say 'slow' or 'behind'. If I feel okay I'll say 'learning disabled'.

A staff member: If people ask me 'How's integration going?' I now think carefully before I answer. I say it differently to different people so that I don't get into knots.

Knowing your own thresholds helps with expansion of thresholds. When a person knows what she wants and what she doesn't want, it is easier for her to set goals, to expand her thresholds and to recognise this expansion when it happens.

A parent: I prefer 'intellectually disabled' or 'developmentally disabled' to 'retarded' because 'retarded' makes me think of institutions. I still have trouble saying 'brain damaged', but I'll get around to it one day.

The strategy of knowing your own thresholds recognises that different people at different times vary in their ability and desire to manage the issues of integration. It also recognises that integration can be stressful. Knowing your own thresholds is a positive strategy that allows a flexible and individual approach to the chances and choices of integration.

Chapter Thirteen

TAKE THE INITIATIVE

Some people are active initiators—they take the lead, make things happen, make the first move. Other people are passive responders—they respond to situations as they happen or to the leads that other people have initiated. Both sorts of people are needed to help make the world go around.

Many people with a disability or parents of children with a disability find that they can easily be responders—other people (usually without disabilities) want to make decisions for them, organise resources, programs or outings for them, or talk on their behalf. People with a disability and their parents sometimes feel that the initiators expect them to be happy and grateful for the passive responding role assigned to them.

However many people are aware that although a passive responding role may be easier much of the time, an active initiating role is often more useful. Trial and error has taught them that taking the initiative provides many advantages, overcomes many difficulties and leaves them feeling more positive and more in control than if they had remained a passive responder.

Taking the initiative is useful for integration; it is a process that can provide people with common ground and an idea of how to talk to, play with or assist a person with a disability. By not sitting back, by taking the initiative, the outcome of integration may be better for everyone than if people had remained passive.

However, taking the initiative can be tiring—it often requires physical and mental energy. Many people with a disability (or their parents) find that they get tired and fed up with having to take the initiative in so many situations. They would love to sit back and always be people at ease, always be able to enjoy everyday experiences, outings and conversations. They would love to have these experiences without needing to initiate moves to be included at all, to put other people at ease and to open the conversation.

It would be wonderful if other people knew that a person with a disability is just a person: you talk with him as you do with other people ('Hello'); you help him in the same way ('Can I help you?'); you work with him similarly ('The canteen is over there, the toilets are to the left, lunch is at 12.15 and Brian is the bloke to see about the football'). Unfortunately not everyone seems to realise this and taking the initiative is one way to help people understand the similarities of all people.

Knowing your own thresholds (chapter 12) may help a person decide whether the advantages of taking the initiative in a particular situation at a particular time outweigh the disadvantages.

Taking the initiative can provide common ground. Staff and parents can choose or suggest activities that provide common ground or shared interests among community members. This can indicate a starting point for a conversation or activity and so facilitate interaction.

> *A parent*: Some children started throwing sand at John, and splashing him to see if he'd react. I let it go for a while and then I said: 'John can't see, but he likes making sand pies'. After that they happily played on the edge of the water for a long time.

Other suggestions include:

- 'Jane likes Frank Sinatra/cheese on toast/ 'Neighbours'/playing cards/ playing the piano.'
- 'John's favourite team/footballer/magazine/food/colour/movie star/ icecream/sport/author is. . . .'
- 'Jane is hoping to go skiing/to the Grand Prix/to a music camp next holidays.'
- 'I saw you reading the computer magazine. I've got an I.B.M. at home I use for. . . .'
- 'I went to the movies/beach/disco/football/park last weekend.'

Taking the initiative can emphasise similarities and 'normality'. Staff and parents sometimes feel annoyed when the achievements of a person with a disability aren't acknowledged or when their similarities with all people are ignored. Sometimes people insist on interpreting the behaviour of a child with a disability in terms of her disability, forgetting that all children can tantrum, bite, throw things and shout. People with a disability may find that everything they say or do is interpreted differently because they have a disability. They are not 'naughty' but 'acting out', not 'bad tempered' but 'maladjusted', not 'pretty' but 'So lucky, she's pretty', not 'naturally charming' but 'well adjusted', not 'selfish' but 'unaware of social opinion', not 'active' but 'physically distractible', not 'polite' but 'learns social skills easily.' They are not 'ordinary' but 'within a normal range', 'within the 17th and the 83rd percentile' or 'within one standard deviation'.

Taking the initiative can bring a person's ordinariness into the conversation by emphasising his similarity to all people—his favourite T.V. program, how she likes her hair done, which teachers he dislikes, which train he catches, part-time jobs, pay-packets, girlfriends.

> *A parent*: In my family Simon is always being asked how he's going at school. I know Simon is very bright and he gets good marks, but I wish someone could ask John how he's going at school. Usually I have to prompt with 'John, bring out the book you're reading—I'm sure everyone would like to see it'.

When other people focus on differences and disabilities, taking the initiative can focus attention back on similarities and abilities.

> *A parent*: I wish some of my friends would ask me other things apart from 'How is she going with that new cup?' or 'How does this wheelchair compare with the last wheelchair?' Jane loves music and has quite a collection of tapes. Just once I wish they'd ask me about her interest in music or which are her favourite T.V. programs. And why don't they comment that it's marvellous to see her choosing her own clothes now? I'm the one who always has to say 'Do you like Jane's haircut? She looked at hundreds of magazines and decided this was the one she liked'.

Taking the initiative can acknowledge differences. Sometimes people seem unable to acknowledge a disability at all. They hide their discomfort by statements like:

- 'What pretty hair.'
- 'What lovely eyes.'
- 'A new watch—how marvellous.'
- 'What a tan—he's been to the beach.'

By taking the initiative and mentioning the disability in passing, it lets other people know that it is alright to talk about it.

- 'It is so noisy here with the stereo on I'd better turn John's hearing aids down. Loud noises can be painful for him.'
- 'Jane loves calisthenics too, but her visual problem means she has to practise a lot at home. When she's here at class she has to really watch the instructors and the other kids to keep up.'

Alternatively a direct statement about the disability can help put people at ease.

- 'I'm getting a new wheelchair next week.'
- 'We're pleased with this caliper—it fits really well.'
- 'I'm on medication for epilepsy and so I can't eat that.'

Direct statements can be used to put people at ease and to acknowledge differences, and their responses may be surprisingly positive.

> *A parent*: Here we were at basketball and this other parent said 'Is yours the other small boy? Mine's the one in the red shirt.' 'Yes,' I said, thinking 'Here we go'. Then she said 'Ronnie's only 6 but those other boys look 8 or 9. How old is your boy?' Long pause and I said '9'. Another long pause and I said 'He's a bit retarded'. No pause at all and she said 'Well this basketball will be good for him'.

Acknowledging the differences can also acknowledge how the differences may affect performance or affect other people in the group. This can still be done while stressing abilities.

> *A person with a disability*: I don't mention my disability when I write job applications. If an interview appointment is made by phone I mention it

then and am very clear about its effect on my work. If I am sent a letter for an interview appointment I mention the same thing early on in the interview. My friend is in a wheelchair and if he gets a letter about an interview appointment he rings to check access to the interview room and mentions his wheelchair then.

A parent: I rang to book my son into beginner's basketball. I told them he was a bit retarded but loved ball games, played goals in the basketball ring at home and knew some of the kids from school in beginner's basketball group.

Taking the initiative can avoid potentially difficult situations. Taking the initiative can be used to avoid conversations and situations that could be difficult.

A sister of a child with a disability: John may have dry skin, but I told Mum that you certainly couldn't send him to school camp with his moisturiser. He'd be laughed at.

Taking the initiative can defuse situations that could become more difficult.

A parent: Mr Leader knew the other parents were angry that the school had an integration teacher. They reckoned we needed a music teacher and another phys. ed. teacher. Well, Mr Leader explained in the school newsletter that there was no choice. The money for specialist teachers came from somewhere else. He also promised to look into phys. ed. too.

A parent: I sometimes say to Susan's friends that John sometimes gets a bit grumpy. It doesn't denigrate him and say that he's a poor disabled kid, but it can acknowledge things and put Susan and her friends at ease.

Taking the initiative can also help people over the difficulty they sometimes have in physically handling people with a disability. Ordinary ways for having physical contact can be suggested.

A parent: When John was a baby, I used to say to visitors 'You hold him and I'll go and put the kettle on'. I'd pass him into their arms and go out to the kitchen. By the time I came back they'd had a chance for a good look, realised he seemed okay even if he was disabled, and that he loved a cuddle. It often seemed to be a big step for them to look directly at him and to physically hold him and this got us both through that.

A parent: I often say 'Can you wipe Jane's nose?' I figure it's something they've done for hundreds of kids and its just the same for Jane. If Jane's nose feels the same as other kids, maybe they won't mind the rest of her, and even give her a cuddle.

Taking the initiative can involve passing on the handy hints that make things work more easily. If the cub leader says 'I'm going to teach all the kids to tie a reef knot', a parent may respond:

- 'If you get John's attention first, he'll be able to lipread you more easily.'
- 'If you remind Jane that her left arm is the one with the watch on, she'll do okay.'

- 'Use a heavy rope for John, rather than a light cord—then his tremor won't interfere so much.'

Taking the initiative can indicate an understanding of other people's perspectives.   By making an offer or passing a comment, a person can indicate an understanding of other people's feelings, an understanding that may be hard to put into words, though the gesture makes it clear.

> *A parent*:   I always ask Jane's teachers if they want me to come down some time and talk to them about Jane. I offer to loan them some books on her condition. They always like that though the poor buggers only realise later that it's the chat that helps them get going, not the book.

> *A parent of a child without a disability*:   I asked Jane's mother if Jane would like to come home after swimming to play with my daughter. She said yes and asked if she could come too. I was relieved she offered to do that.

Taking the initiative can be used to 'shape' people's responses.   Taking the initiative can give feedback to people, and 'shape' their responses towards preferred words and behaviour. It can help other people use attitudes and behaviour that support integration. A positive response to people's appropriate behaviour makes them more likely to repeat those words and deeds again. In this way their responses can be gradually shaped.

- 'I'm glad you make Jane sit at the table for her drink. Some of my friends let kids wander with their drinks, but I think it is important that Jane learns good habits early on.'
- 'I'm glad I'm not the only one who thinks John needs a firm hand; everyone except you and I seems to let him get away with murder.'

Responding to people's behaviour gives them a better idea of how to interact; they are not left 'fishing' for the right thing to do. They are helped even further when they receive not only a positive response to their past behaviour, but also suggestions about other situations in which to use that behaviour, and about other similar behaviours that are appropriate.

- 'I'm glad you stop Jane interrupting conversations. I'm trying to stop her wanting immediate attention too, like when she calls out from the other side of the classroom.'
- 'I'm glad you enjoy giving John a cuddle; he loves affection. I try to give him cuddles, kisses or hugs rather than rocking him as he rocks a lot on his own, and it's becoming a habit I'm trying to break.'

Many people feel that particular words affect other people's attitudes and that using the right words can encourage better attitudes to integration. Not all people like the same words, but some words certainly seem to have less stigma attached. People's responses can be shaped towards the preferred words by repeating other people's correct choice of words.

- *Statement*: 'How did Jane become spastic?'
- *Response*: 'Jane's been spastic since the car accident when she was two.'

If non-preferred words are used by other people, they can be replaced with preferred words with the hope that the speaker will take the hint and re-use the preferred words.

- *Statement*: 'I knew another mongol who could speak really well.'
- *Response*: 'Yes, many people with Down syndrome can speak well.'

Taking the initiative is a positive interpersonal strategy. It provides a way to not only react to events and make the best of them, but also to take control of situations and to promote attitudes that will make integration work.

Chapter Fourteen

USE HUMOUR

Many people believe that interaction with or conversation about people who have a disability should only be done very solemnly or with an air of tragedy. They are therefore surprised when people with a disability or their parents don't always have the same attitude. They are sometimes bewildered when these people make statements which seem irreverent, flippant or (gasp!) even amusing. What they probably find hard to understand is that it is possible for the parents of a child with a disability to have continuing feelings of sadness about their child, but still be able to use humour constructively. Similarly people with a disability can at different times feel sad, angry, disappointed or frustrated with their disability but at other times still be amused by their disability and the predicaments into which it gets them.

It is certainly up to people with a disability or their parents to initiate the use of humour; it is not the prerogative of other people to make jokes about disabilities or about people with a disability.

Humour lightens situations and puts people at ease. Humour can help manage some potentially uncomfortable situations.

> *A parent*: I was once with a group of friends and the conversation got around to what each other's children were going to do when they left school. Everyone chatted on for a while and it seemed that everyone's child was going to be a doctor, a dentist, a vet or a lawyer. After a while voices started to trail off and there was this rather uncomfortable silence and some embarrassed glances in my direction. In a cheery voice I said 'John wants to be a pilot.' (John actually does want to be a pilot— although we haven't disillusioned him yet). There was a stunned silence and when they saw me laughing, they all relaxed and we actually talked about the topic for the first time.

> *A parent*: I sometimes tell people that we had thought of calling her Melody, but were glad we hadn't when we found out later that she was deaf.

Humour diffuses an air of tragedy. Humour can diffuse the air of tragedy that often surrounds a person with a disability and their families; it allows people to laugh together at a situation (not at a person).

A parent: I sometimes say 'Oh well, a long tongue is good for some things'.

Humour can be part of a prepared short answer. (chapter 16) Sometimes humour in a prepared short answer makes a point and relieves embarrassment on the part of other people. A prepared humourous short answer to frequently recurring situations can leave a person feeling more in control than if she'd answered in an ad hoc way.

A parent: If we bump into people and they angrily say 'Watch out', I say 'Sorry, it's the blind leading the blind'.

Humour can avoid an outburst of anger. Anger can leave people feeling distressed and may do nothing to help them reach their goal of making integration work. Humour can be used to defuse the current situation but also provide time to prepare a more assertive response to use later (chapter 15).

A parent: I often use humourous self-talk in my mind when I really think I'll blow—'I must look like a cross between a steam roller and a pressure cooker'.

Humour provides a balance. Humour can balance the sadness that people with a disability or their parents may feel against the knowledge that a lot of their life is very normal and in fact humourous. Some parents have a store of humourous incidents which they relate as needed: the time John got stuck in the ashtray in the doctor's waiting room, the time the brake went on the wheelchair and someone was knocked into the street procession, the time he popped his glass eye out in the supermarket, the time he vomitted into someone's handbag on the train. The fact is, of course, that all of these incidents were very difficult when they happened, but in retelling they seem more bearable.

A parent: When I made his cake for his seventh birthday I accidentally made a backward 'seven' shape. I often tell people because it lets them see that I can laugh about it though I also often let them know that I wept buckets of tears at the time, too.

Humour is an interpersonal strategy that some people find easier to use than others. It is an extremely effective way to demonstrate a personal perspective on disability and integration without using complicated statements or taking an aggressive stand.

Chapter Fifteen

BE ASSERTIVE

'Be assertive' is one of the catchphrases of the late 1970s and 1980s. It is used in business ('Don't be passed over for promotion—develop your assertive skills'); in consumer affairs ('Be assertive—don't put up with faulty goods and poor service'); and in interpersonal relations ('Know your rights and responsibilities—become assertive').

Many people involved with integration—parents, staff, community members and people with a disability—are aware that their interactions are not always easy and also that sometimes they don't have the desired effect. People may recognise their differing viewpoints and feelings about integration and its success, and also recognise that these differences contribute to their discomfort and to the ineffectiveness of some of their communications. They may recognise the value of good communication, but find that honest, rational communication in integration is often difficult.

> *A parent*: I've had more to do with my child's development than other parents have; I know him well. But I don't know how to tell the teacher what I know.

Many people wish they could handle interactions more comfortably and effectively. They want to lessen strained feelings, tense meetings and bitter arguments, yet these same people may dismiss using assertion to improve their interactions because they don't want to, or feel they can't, be more assertive.

People often misunderstand the meaning of assertion, believing it to be unnatural, insincere, impolite and complicated. They think that assertion involves anger, arguments, criticism, and having to use particular words or phrases; they think it means completely changing the way they currently deal with conflict.

> I don't want to be more assertive. I hate it when people are angry at me and I don't want to yell at them either.

> I just can't be assertive.... The only time I'm assertive is in the car by myself where I have imaginary conversations with people.

> I think being assertive is a good theory but it is not for me. I can't face a problem head on, instead I find other ways around it...Saying those things is not the way I speak, and even if I practised I'd be so nervous I'd pack up.

This poor understanding of assertion no doubt contributes to people's reluctance to consider being more assertive.

THE NATURE OF ASSERTION

Being assertive means being aware of your own rights and expressing your thoughts and feelings in direct, honest ways that do not ignore the rights of other people. The goals of assertion are giving and getting respect, asking for fair play and leaving room for compromise. It may help to think of assertion as the middle ground between non-assertion and aggression.

Assertion is not limited only to areas of conflict. Being assertive provides a basis for any sort of communication (a passing comment, an important statement, words of advice or an expressed viewpoint) with any sort of person (a close friend, an acquaintance, a group of people, committee members, a stranger, a colleague, a care provider or a parent). Assertion avoids both a 'right or wrong' approach and a 'win or lose' approach; it is important to realise that by being assertive a person may not necessarily get his own way but then again, he may do so.

Because assertion leaves room for compromise and for different people's viewpoints, it can stop a person feeling swayed by the offers, efforts and feelings of other people, even those of 'do-gooders'. Assertion allows a person to listen to other people's comments and recognise their efforts, but also to realise that other people's good intentions need not lead to a feeling of indebtedness.

Assertion is an attitude just as much as it is a type of behaviour. A person's attitude towards someone may change through her understanding of assertion—she may realise that other people have a right to an opinion and to different opinions. This changed perception may defuse what appeared to be an insensitive comment: if a friend says 'I think John would be better off at a residential unit' a parent may be deeply hurt unless she realises that the friend is expressing his opinion with no guilt or blame intended.

An understanding of the true meaning of assertion is important, because despite the stated reluctance of many people to use assertion, the truth is that a simple assertive statement can give people what they want from communications—comfortable, useful interactions that achieve their purpose.

BECOMING MORE ASSERTIVE

Assertive communications are based on a number of strategies. They can be practised individually, used in the sequence outlined or used in a general way.

Become aware of situations where you don't express feelings or opinions easily. Identify specific situations (perhaps meetings, interviews or decision-making) where being assertive is particularly difficult. Some people find that a particular person's presence makes it difficult to be assertive, no matter the nature of the situation.

State clearly how you feel. This must be done without placing blame on other people and may be done most easily by using a sentence starting with 'I'.

- 'I always feel so happy to see Jane and Susan playing together.'

Positive feelings may be easier to express than negative feelings, however negative feelings may be easier to express than imagined if no blame for those feelings is placed on the other person:

- 'I feel upset when I realise that no matter how well you teach John, he'll never learn to read', rather than 'You'll never teach John to read.'
- 'I feel confused when you tell me, Mr Staff, that John will never get a full-time job yet the foreman tells me he's working well', rather than 'You always say something different to everyone else and none of you seems to know what you are doing.'
- 'I feel worried that Jane doesn't get as much help with her work here as she would at a special school.'
- 'I am worried that my child doesn't get the attention she needs and has a right to.'

It often helps other people to pay attention if such statements about feelings are *preceded by acknowledgment of the other person's feelings:*

- 'I know you feel more comfortable when we go to the epilepsy meetings together, Paul, but I don't feel like going tonight.'

Acknowledging the other person's feelings shows a recognition of their right to have differing feelings, and this can be particularly useful where viewpoints are strongly opposed.

- 'Paul, I know you want John to brush his own teeth, but he's so unreliable that I think we should help him.'
- 'Pam, I know that you like to take Jane to watch Sally play basketball but she gets uncomfortable in the wheelchair for so long and the cold bothers her. I'd prefer her to develop a leisure interest of her own rather than tag along to Sally's basketball.'

Acknowledgment of the other person's feelings gives a message of 'I feel upset/uncomfortable when you say/do that', rather than 'You are mean/hurtful/wrong to say/do that.'

If a person doesn't express their irritation or disapproval of other people's words or actions, those people may presume that their words or actions are acceptable. They are likely to repeat them, and so cause more discomfort and tension than if an initial response of disapproval had been expressed.

Set limits for yourself and for other people. Knowing your own thresholds (chapter 12) helps a person identify the limits to the time and effort she is prepared to give towards helping integration work.

- 'I can help on either Thursday mornings or Tuesday afternoons, but not both times.'

Setting limits also makes it easier to say 'No' to the demands of other people.

- 'I won't be going to the meeting tonight.'
- 'I can't provide lunch at the working bee on Saturday.'
- 'I won't be able to donate the drinks to the dinner dance again this year.'
- 'I won't be able to provide help more than once a month.'

A reason for the limit need not be given, as a person should not feel compelled to defend his right to do and say as he likes, providing he doesn't interfere with the rights of other people.

If a person agrees to something she doesn't like, she may feel angry with herself and resentful of other people. By *not* setting limits, through subtle gestures she may give other people a message of unfriendliness and unco-operativeness. This is the same message that she initially worried she would give if she *did* set limits. When a person sets limits, she is teaching other people how to treat her—directly, as distinct from in an unfriendly or unco-operative way.

State clearly what you want. People may think they know other people's preferences and the help they would like, but they may be wrong. Honest, direct statements avoid confusion and presumption; the responsibility to clearly state what they want lies with each person.

- 'I prefer to use the words "cerebral palsy" to "spastic".'
- 'It would be such a help to me if you commented on Susan's performance even though it is a different standard to the other kids' in your group.'
- 'I'd prefer help for a double session once a fortnight, rather than a short session once a week.'
- 'The most pressing need is for someone to investigate the best computer options and adapted programs. Can you do that?'

    A parent: I told the staff that I didn't want Sally to be given any more responsibility for Jane than other older sisters.

Other people may pay more attention if statements about wants are *preceded by acknowledgment of other people's efforts.*

- 'Mr Staff, you did a great job fitting out the workplace here so that John is independent—I reckon that you're really good with technical things. Could you also look at the best sort of headpiece for John to use on the typewriter?'

Acknowledgment of other people's efforts indicates an appreciation of their efforts and desire to help. It is then easier to acknowledge any comments and behaviours which were not appreciated—a message of 'I like you (or some aspects of you), but not what you are saying or doing in this instance.'

- 'I know how much you and Mr Leader have helped all the people here at school to accept Jane, however, I feel uncomfortable when I hear you describe Jane as "spastic". I know she has spasms in her muscles, but I prefer the words "cerebral palsy". Could you use the words "cerebral palsy" when talking about Jane, please? It would mean a lot to me to know that you were helping other people understand the cause of Jane's problems.'

- 'Mr Leader, I want to thank you for organising the camp so that there was plenty for Jane to do. It was great. I am a bit concerned, though, at how cheeky she's become since she got home. It may be that she thinks the informality of camp is okay at home, too. Please don't encourage her to keep on with this "Howdy doody everyone" thing—it is quite out of place in church and school assembly. I think she is quite capable of realising there are different rules for different places, and I'd appreciate it if you'd help reinforce that for her.'

By clearly stating what is wanted, a person keeps the situation more practical than emotional. Rather than only stating feelings about what has been said/done, constructive alternatives have been identified.

USING ASSERTION

Assertive communications have a role in most aspects of integration. It is only if people do communicate clearly and assertively that perspectives and opinions can be recognised, common ground be discovered and fair negotiations take place.

Assertive communications can outline a dilemma. Outlining the dilemma can be useful in situations where a person feels somewhat trapped. It gives people a more complete understanding of the problem and thus helps them see different points of view more fully. It hopefully prompts them to take action that is acceptable to everyone.

> *A parent*: I had to tell Mr Staff that we find it tricky to know how to handle Susan sometimes. The difficulty is that she is very precious to us and we want to let her know that; but we don't know how to show her this without spoiling her rotten.

Assertion can be used to provide some ground rules. Ground rules to common situations can be particularly useful with people who have very entrenched personalities and who have given no indication that they are going to change.

- 'We have a morning tea roster for everyone that uses this lunch room.'
- 'Everyone gets a turn to pick the television program.'
- 'Everyone takes their turn drying the dishes.'
- 'Each person will have equal time on the computer.'

Many parents use assertive statements to clearly establish with staff the relationship they wish to have with the community—the limits to the type and amount of efforts they are prepared to make.

Assertive communications encourage effective decision-making. Effective integration often requires meetings to reach decisions about common goals, programs and resources, and so effective integration requires effective decisions. An effective decision-making process (chapter 10) considers the opinions of all the members contributing to that decision, and allows discussion of those various opinions until a decision acceptable to all members is reached. Thus, effective decision-making requires rational, clear, non-judgemental communications (assertive communications) so that discussion can lead to a decision.

By being assertive—stating clearly how you feel, setting limits for yourself and other people and stating clearly what you want—a person leaves no doubt or confusion in the minds of other people. They know how he feels, what he wants and what he doesn't want. With this information the whims of personalities and the disappointment of wrong presumptions can be avoided; people have information to implement the individual opinions, chances and choices that make integration work.

Chapter Sixteen

USE ROLE PLAY AND SELF-TALK

Many people clearly recall details of upsetting incidents from the past; they can go through situations line by line, sometimes re-experiencing the same emotions. In recalling these incidents, they may also add lines that they could have said. There is often a feeling of 'If only I had said this and this and this. . .'. Similarly people often anticipate conversations and situations they will face in the future, sometimes even imagining quite complicated details. They may vary the words and reactions of the various 'players' in their mind, including their own role.

Role play and self-talk are two techniques used to help a person prepare for and manage potentially difficult situations. Both techniques help people manage their emotions, and communicate effectively and confidently.

ROLE PLAY

Role play prepares a person for situations by having them go through their 'role' before the situation arises and thus before their role is needed. Practice can help people feel more confident when situations do arise and when they need their practiced role. Certainly many incidents are totally unexpected, but various versions of the same difficult interactions do recur.

PRACTISING ROLE PLAY

Role play can be practised with the help of a friend. A friend, colleague or partner can act out an identified situation and play 'opposite' the person wanting to practise their role. The friend can provide a variety of statements and responses as the practice situation develops, so that the person is well prepared when the situation occurs in real life.

Practising role play can help with many situations and people:

- A parent-teacher interview.
- A discussion with the headmaster or club leader.
- A doctor's appointment.
- The over-generous man in the café.
- The nosy next door neighbour.

- Family get-togethers.
- The initial visit to the local playgroup with a child who has a disability.
- The rude child living in the street.
- Offering help to a neighbour who has a disability.

Role play can be practised alone. A person can practise role play alone by imagining a situation and trying out various responses—in a mirror, out loud, into a tape recorder, written down or silently (though silently is not as good practice as the other ways).

> *A parent*: Before I go, I write down all the questions I want to ask and memorise them. I write down all the questions he might ask me and the statements he might make and I rehearse my replies to those too. I also practise saying 'Could you tell me what that means, Mr Leader?' for when he uses words I can't understand.

Practising responses and statements is useful, but the best practice is in real life; the responses and statements need to be ultimately used in the situations for which they were intended, not forever in practice. Practice responses are often not perfect and so their use in real situations may indicate new and better ways to respond.

USING ROLE PLAY

Role play can keep emotions in check. Role play can help a person keep emotions in check by removing some of the element of surprise which can otherwise intensify emotions. Surprise usually allows people no chance to weigh the pros and cons of a response, to consider other people's perspectives or to draw on past experience. Lack of opportunity to do these things can lead to an emotional outburst that is more intense than intended or that doesn't reflect true feelings.

Role play can be a step towards a solution. Role play can be used to practise other interpersonal techniques like taking the initiative (chapter 13), using humour (chapter 14) and being assertive (chapter 15).

Role play can be used to rehearse a short answer. Role play is particularly effective in rehearsing a short answer to commonly recurring questions. People with a disability, their families and carers often get frustrated by the same questions and comments; they find it very useful to have a rehearsed short answer that they can use as needed.

A range of short answers can be prepared to meet varying audiences—a brusque answer for nosy strangers, a more friendly and informed answer for people who obviously care and a simple response for children's questions.

- 'They are hearing aids. John wears them to make sounds louder for him, just as you can turn up the volume on the T.V.'

- 'The therapist thinks that Jane will learn to walk, but she may still need to use a wheelchair for long distances.'
- 'Yes, John is musical but so is the whole family. It's not because he's got Down syndrome; it's a family interest in music.'
- 'It's sad that John is disabled, but he is happy.'

Humour can be part of an effective short answer for some audiences (chapter 14).

Parents can sometimes help staff develop their own short answers, enabling them to feel confident and prepared in an area where perhaps they would otherwise feel vulnerable and unsure.

> *A parent:* I often suggest to staff that they tell other kids that Jane's legs don't work too well, but that her hands are great and she does fantastic drawings.

SELF-TALK

Most people have statements that they say sub-consciously to themselves. Some of these can be useful and encouraging ('I think this person likes me') and others can be detrimental and discouraging ('I bet the dentist will hurt today').

No matter their intent, the words people say to themselves (self-talk) affect their attitudes to themselves, to a situation and to other people. In recalling or anticipating incidents, people often use sub-conscious phrases that judge themselves ('He admired me when I did that' or 'I looked foolish'); that judge the situation ('It never works') or that judge other people ('She's set against this'). If they say 'I'm no good at this' then they are less likely to become good at it; if they say 'Integration will never work' then it is less likely to work; if they say 'This person doesn't want integration to work' then they will blindly interpret that person's behaviour in that way.

The technique of self-talk takes statements out of the sub-conscious and assesses their usefulness. The statements are then used, changed or replaced so that they provide the most help for particular situations.

Because integration is new and unfamiliar to some people, they may use the negative self-talk common to unfamiliar situations—'I've never done this before', 'I don't know what to do', 'This isn't fair', 'I can't manage', 'Other people can do this better'. Using self-talk is particularly useful in integration to ensure that the sub-conscious phrases people use are positive and helpful, rather than negative and destructive.

USING SELF-TALK

Self-talk can provide a sense of confidence. Self-talk can prepare a person for a situation and put her in a positive frame of mind.

- 'I managed last time.'
- 'I've got some ideas to offer here. I can help.'

- 'This will be good experience for next time.'
- 'I never expect anything too much, so anything good is a bonus.'

Self-talk can provide a perspective on a situation. Self-talk can be used as a reminder of other people's perspectives, as an attempt to understand their position or at least to acknowledge that they have a different perspective:

- 'She has a right to her opinion.'
- 'She is just as nervous as me.'
- 'My suggestions are as important as other people's.'
- 'He's doing the wrong thing but for the right reasons.'
- 'They don't know any better.'
- 'We're all in this together.'
- 'She feels anxious, that's why she's saying those things.'
- 'Is that what she really means? I don't think so.'
- 'Now, if I was him, what would I think?'
- 'I wonder why he said that?'
- 'It must be different for them.'

Self-talk can sometimes stop a sense of panic:

- 'Things could be worse.'
- 'This is not the first time that this has happened and it won't be the last.'
- 'Nothing is forever.'
- 'This moment will soon be over.'
- 'How important is this in the scale of things?'

Self-talk can be used as a reminder of personal perspectives and personal goals.

- 'Is this important enough to be getting so upset?'
- 'Don't get upset over small things.'
- 'Is this worrying me more than John?'
- 'Will this matter in the long run?'
- 'I'm never going to see this person again, so why bother?'
- 'If I blow up, I'll be the one upset, not her.'

Self-talk can help keep emotions in check. It is not always advantageous to keep emotions in check, but it can prevent people saying or doing something that they regret; it can also prevent them acting or speaking in a harsher way than they intended. Self-talk can sometimes be used in the short-term, to get through difficult moments—perhaps to keep anger from spilling over and thus provide time to develop a more assertive response, some ground rules (chapter 15) or a rehearsed short answer:

- 'I'll bite my tongue.'
- 'It's nearly over.'
- 'He doesn't really mean that.'
- 'Plug on. Don't blow up.'

Sometimes, self-talk keeps emotions in check sufficiently to then allow acknowledgment of people's different perspectives.

- 'Don't crack—that's what he wants me to do.'
- 'What's the point—he's never going to change.'

Role play and self-talk are techniques that people commonly use both in difficult situations ('What will I do if he says that?') and in exciting situations ('I want to see their faces when I tell them that we've won'). Because these techniques are familiar (even if people have never put the names of 'role play' and 'self-talk' on them) they are good starting points in managing the personal interactions of integration.

Chapter Seventeen

EVALUATION

This book has frequently mentioned the phrase 'making integration work'. This phrase implies that somewhere clear definitions exist of terms like: 'integration that is working', 'good integration' and 'bad integration'. Unfortunately this is not so.

People often attempt to evaluate integration in an effort to define these terms; they also attempt to define these terms in an effort to evaluate integration. The definitions need the evaluation and the evaluation needs the definition—they are intertwined. Many people want answers to questions like: What is integration that works? What does it look like? How does it feel to staff, parents, community members and people with a disability? How do you know when it is happening? How can you make it happen? People want to know about their own particular community: Is integration working? How well is it working? Why is it working or not working?

People evaluate many situations that affect them—friendships, jobs or tax changes. They do this in order to understand the situation's effect on them and perhaps to decide whether they will continue their involvement with, discard or attempt to modify the situation. People particularly evaluate situations in which they have played a part. This is understandable as they often want to know how successful or influential their role has been. Similarly many people who have put an effort into making integration work want to know how it is going. However people's reasons for evaluating integration vary. Some want to keep integration working, to help integration to work, to identify its success; some may want to provide evidence of integration's failure and a reason to ignore it.

People most commonly evaluate situations from a personal perspective. Thus people evaluate integration based on their own involvement with, or perceptions of, integration and these perceptions and involvements will vary. People value different aspects of their community and of their lives and so will see integration, its effects and 'success' differently.

Integration may therefore be judged 'successful' for some people but not for others, 'successful' by some people and not by others, 'successful' in some aspects and not in others, or 'successful' at some times but not others. If normalisation (chapter 2) is taken seriously, then the perception of success that is held by the person who has the disability is very important.

Evaluation of integration is not simple. Any information from an evaluation is only as good as the evaluation process used. A sound evaluation will produce useful information; a poor evaluation will produce useless information. A good evaluation requires knowing exactly what is being evaluated so that the most appropriate evaluation process can be used. It is important to differentiate between evaluation of the process of integration in a community, particular programs used, and a person's performance. These are three entirely different types of evaluation and must be treated as such.

EVALUATING THE PROCESS OF INTEGRATION IN A COMMUNITY

Integration is no different to other social processes in a community. It is no less likely to happen or to work or to become accepted than other social processes. 'The vote for women' and 'migrant assimilation' probably seemed just as radical ideas in their times and were fraught with just as many differing opinions and difficulties as is integration today.

Integration is a social process that can be evaluated like other social processes, but it does not need to be evaluated to justify it; integration is justified, without qualification, as a process of social justice. Evaluation of integration does not imply that it can be discarded if found to be working poorly. Evaluation implies a review of the process used by the community to make integration work; evaluation should be used to provide information to make integration more successful, to make it a stronger force towards social justice in that community. Good evaluation doesn't ask 'Can integration be kept going?' but instead asks 'How can integration be kept going?'

Unfortunately, integration is not an either...or situation where either it is undeniably happening or it is not happening at all. (A pity, because that would certainly make it easier to evaluate). Integration cannot be predicted or evaluated by paperwork or by looking at facts and figures; neither the person's degree of disability, the community's experience with integration or the variety of available resources are good predictors of the success of the person's integration.

Integration can't be judged by appearances; the observation that a teenager is wearing Op-shop clothes indicates neither that integration is happening nor that it isn't happening (chapter 1). It is the process that leads the teenager to wear the Op-shop clothes that is the indicator of integration. Similarly the presence of expensive or high-technology resources doesn't mean that good integration processes are being used. It is the process of appropriately choosing and using the resources that is the indicator of integration.

Integration is a process that sometimes takes a while to have an effect or to show its full effect, and sometimes it is difficult to see that effect. A small change (like learning to use public transport) can have a large effect on one aspect of a person's choices in a community, even though much of their life may still be spent in a segregated community where it appears they have only limited chances and choices. A person in a well equipped and well staffed segregated accommodation unit could, in fact, have more choices than a similarly disabled person in an ordinary house with no specialised equipment and with insufficient staff to allow individual time-tables and routines, likes and dislikes, choices or variety.

Like all social processes, integration is difficult to define and to evaluate because it is a process not a state; it will be implemented differently in different communities and at different times. However its basic principles (social justice, equal opportunity, non-categorisation and non-segregation) remain the same. If integration looks different in different communities, it just means that a community is applying the principles of integration to its own unique community, programs, people, facilities and resources.

Because integration is not static, it may not be a resounding success initially, just as a job or marriage may not. The success of integration can change (just as the success of and satisfaction with a job or marriage changes); it is because it can change that evaluation is important. Evaluation can provide information that helps the process of integration in a community change and become more successful.

Evaluating the process of integration in a community requires observations about the community's functioning and about the processes it uses to fulfil the needs of its members. Particular observations indicate that good processes have been used to lead to good outcomes for all the community's members.

Successful integration is based on positive attitudes. Successful communities don't question integration, though community members may question the suitability of a particular program or the effect of particular attitudes. They recognise difficulties as problems to be overcome rather than as impenetrable obstacles. Successful communities use problem-solving processes (chapter 10) to make integration work because they know it can work. They know that integration is influenced more by the attitudes both of individual people and of the media than by laws and policies.

> *A staff member:* Resources and hardware are not easy but at least they are clearcut. It is shifting attitudes that is the crux of integration.

Successful integration stays below community consciousness. Successful communities recognise that positive attitudes towards integration can be low-key. Integration can be in the background, not a foreground issue; integration can become part of the regular functioning of the community. Integration implies acceptance of a person and her disability—assimilating her, her way of life, her choices, her abilities and her individuality into a community whose members have a wide range of lifestyles choices and abilities. Community members can then begin to see individual people, not disabilities.

> *A parent:* My son has Down syndrome, glasses and a hearing aid. He also had a limp from a broken leg when he started at the school. At the end of the year, one of his friends asked why he still had his integration

Attendance at a community

aide because 'He doesn't limp anymore'. This boy had seen John's 'difference' as the limp, not all the other bits and pieces us adults would see.

Successful integration means participation.   Successful communities
recognise that integration means more than just attendence at the community. It means a person with a disability participates in a community's
programs and is involved with its resources.

Successful integration means interaction.   Successful communities
recognise that interaction between community members deepens the integration that community attendance and program participation has initiated. The best resources, facilities and programs can provide choices but
only interaction between community members can provide a sense of
'belonging'.

Successful integration means interdependence.   Successful communities support the interdependence of community members, encouraging them to both assist and depend on each other.

Successful integration is ongoing.   Successful communities recognise
that integration is not static. It is neither 'a current project', nor 'a problem'
nor 'a situation'. It is a process that is ongoing, that can be planned for,
nurtured and influenced by efforts and attitudes. Indeed, it needs ongoing
nurturing to continue to be successful.

Successful integration recognises success—wherever it is.   Successful communities are just as happy to judge the success of their integration

processes by the 'naughty but normal' things as by the 'clever, goal-oriented' things.

> *A parent*: I knew integration was working for Jane when she skipped school. Wheelchair and all, she just skipped school and went to town on the train. I didn't know whether to laugh or cry.

> *A parent*: I knew integration was working when John learnt a dirty joke. He certainly hadn't been taught that by the teachers. He could only have learnt it from other kids, and that's what he was integrated for—to learn all the things that kids learn, not just the good.

Successful integration values the unexpected. Successful communities are just as thrilled by unplanned positive outcomes as those they've consciously worked towards.

> *A parent*: I knew integration was working when John had friends that I didn't know about and that I hadn't organised.

> *A teacher*: He's lost weight since he's been here at school with us. We certainly hadn't planned that, but it's great.

Successful integration considers the whole community. Successful communities recognise that social processes can't be judged by looking at a couple of people. Successful communities recognise the influence of integration on all community members, not just on members who have a disability.

Successful integration responds to community members' needs. Successful communities don't have rigid, outdated standards that members must abide by, but instead are able to change their programs and expectations to respond to the needs of their members.

Successful integration values the development of people. Successful communities recognise that ordinary events and remarks may indicate success for a person with a disability though they may be insignificant to other people.

> *A parent*: A parent of a regular child told me that her boy and mine had got into trouble yesterday for giggling. The two best things were that it was an ordinary thing to get into trouble for, and best of all, she didn't tell me that John had got her boy into trouble. She'd said 'They got into trouble together.' I knew then that integration was worthwhile.

Successful integration uses teamwork. Successful communities share responsibility for integration among a team of flexible people. They also recognise that staff and other community members may need support to plan and implement an integration program, and so they provide high-quality preparation, ongoing education and support networks. They use good communication and effective decision-making to ensure genuine teamwork.

EVALUATING INTEGRATION PROGRAMS

A specific integration program is easier to evaluate than the process of integration in a community. This is particularly true if the program has been developed (as it should have been) around goals and objectives, and has resulted in an individual integration program designed for a specific person. Well written objectives contain information on *who* will do *what* under *what conditions, how well* and by *when*. The success of the program is then evaluated by examining whether that person has made progress towards or has met those goals and objectives using those conditions.

The fact that an integration program of any sort even exists indicates that at least a minimum of planning has happened. This is a favourable sign because planning (preferably early, detailed, collaborative planning—chapter 6) is quoted again and again as an important factor for successful integration.

Information from evaluation of an integration program should be used to make the program more successful. Evaluation shouldn't be used to show that the program didn't work and therefore integration can't happen. Information showing a program's difficulties simply indicates that this program wasn't as successful as expected. Another program—using different materials or resources, using changed format and content—may be very successful.

The program checklist (chapter 8) and resource checklist (chapter 9) can be used to evaluate the appropriateness of the program with respect to the individual for whom it was developed.

- Program goals and objectives are community-referenced.
- The program content is the least restrictive.
- The program format is the least restrictive.
- Community-referenced instruction is used.
- The resources used are tied to resource needs.
- Resource needs are community-referenced.
- The least restrictive resource type is used.
- The chosen resource is used in the least restrictive way.
- Resources complement each other.

There are additional factors to consider in evaluating how successful the individual integration program has been or is likely to be:

Program decisions are based on the notion of social justice. The program recognises the needs of all community members. Resources are allocated and access to programs is provided on the basis that all people have equal value and the same rights.

The program is developed and implemented through co-operation. Collaborative decision-making (chapter 10) is used to develop consensus decisions that are co-operatively implemented. The individual planning committee is broad based—many people share both program decisions and responsibility for implementing them. They have a common understanding about the goals of this program for this person (and thus the goals of integration for this person).

Program objectives are clearly defined.   Program objectives are clear enough to allow progress towards them to be clearly identified.

The program has flexible assessment criteria.   The program uses individual assessment criteria that are functional. A product, some answers, or skill development may not be necessary as proof of the program's value. But assessment processes do indicate that the program has helped the person with the disability to progress towards his objective.

The program encourages independence.   The program has goals of increased independence of both thought and action. Programs allow risks and choices, and allow a balance between protection and self-determination (chapter 10) in order to promote the development of independence.

EVALUATING A PERSON (ASSESSMENT PROCESSES)

For many parents of a child with a disability, 'assessment' is a dreaded word. For them, 'assessment' has usually been done countless times before by countless different people for countless different reasons (and sometimes for countless unknown reasons too!). They may fear 'assessment' because, for their child, it has often been associated with eligibility for a particular service.

In integration, assessment or evaluation of a person has nothing to do with 'eligibility' or 'readiness' for integration. Neither should it be confused with an evaluation of integration processes or integration programs.

Assessment information about a person's abilities and difficulties can be used for both planning and evaluating an individual integration program. Assessment should focus on a person's skills and abilities, and take note of any difficulties which may prevent her full participation in the community. Good assessment has an outcome that lists actions to be undertaken to allow more interaction, fuller participation and more chances and choices. Assessment should be an instructional device to help staff devise a better program, not a way of deciding who is worthy of teaching. Assessment's role is not to exclude people but to provide information to better include people. It should not be used to categorise a person but to increase his participation, not to find an appropriate placement but to find an appropriate program, not just to establish differences but also to foster abilities.

Assessment may not tell a lot about a person except that they could or couldn't do that test on that day in that way. Good assessment is repeated and varied to discover if on another day or with material presented in another way, a person's performance could be different. This information

Participation in a community's activities

is then used to develop overall goals or short-term objectives that will become part of an individual program.

Good assessment allows a variety of ways of reaching an objective—ways that reflect a person's likes, dislikes, skills and difficulties. A specific response or a given score are not the only correct indicators that a goal has been reached. A score or mark can indicate change, growth or that an objective has been reached, but so can particular behaviour or language, or a variety of other responses. If the objective is that a child will hit two hand-held objects together, it doesn't matter whether he bangs together two blocks, two plastic rings or two brussel sprouts.

Assessment is only useful if an appropriate person does an appropriate form of assessment that provides wanted information and if the information is used.

Community-referenced assessment provides functional information about abilities. *Norm-referenced assessments*—standardised assessments where a person's performance is compared to that of a norm (the performance of an average person)—may provide information that is generally obvious. Norm-referenced assessment information is presented in a comparative way: 'She is reading at a grade 2 level'; 'His work output is 40% of normal'. Norm-referenced assessments can provide information for program planning or setting objectives: 'So, John can't stack seven blocks like most nine year olds? Then we'd better teach him. That can be an objective.' or 'Jane's general knowledge is below the norm for a teenage girl? Then we'd better get her to read the newspaper more often.' However objectives developed from norm-referenced assessments may not be relevant to the person's lifestyle or interests, or to the community; they may be far removed from the person's abilities. If John can't stack two blocks because of a physical disability, stacking seven blocks is impossible, and how relevant to his ultimate lifestyle is stacking anyway?

Community-referenced assessments may be more useful. They use a person's actual abilities and needs in a particular community to assess performance: 'She has a sight vocabulary that includes her family's and classmates' names, road signs, shop names and her bus stop'; 'His work output improved 20% with alterations to his workstation layout, and another 20% when the piecework bonus system was explained to him'. They provide criteria important to that person in that community rather than norms of what most people can do but which don't relate to a particular community. More importantly, community-referenced assessments provide information about skills that are familiar and relevant to the person who has the disability, rather than skills which have a known 'normal performance' but may be unfamiliar or irrelevant to a particular person. Jane may not be up-to-date in general knowledge, but of greater value to her integration (to her interaction with her peers) may be her knowledge about pop singers, skateboards, hair-crimpers and discos.

Descriptive assessment provides quality information about performance. An individual planning committee may find it difficult to evaluate a person's performance if both the content of the program and the process of learning are different to that used by other community members, or if formal evaluation processes that are familiar to the program designers are not possible for this particular program. Descriptive assessment may overcome some of these difficulties.

Descriptive assessment describes a person's work in an objective, detailed and value-free way by focusing on what the person has done and what she can do. 'Has done' means an account of the learning experiences, and 'can do' means the specific qualities of the person's work—the skills and abilities that the person has demonstrated. Thus, when someone reads a descriptive assessment he knows what goes on in that program and what the person's work is like.

Descriptive assessment describes a person's growth and learning, 'using either that student's own previous work or the stipulated goals of the program (as a measure of growth) or both: never the performance of other students'.[14] It is a non-competitive, non-graded assessment that is more informative than marks or assessment ratings—it is objective while still allowing for individual differences between people.

Evaluation is a difficult but vital part of making integration work. Evaluation of the integration processes in a community provides information to support the programs that make integration work; evaluation of a person's performance provides information to modify the programs; and evaluation of the programs provides information to develop better programs that let integration be even more successful.

Chapter Eighteen

TROUBLESHOOTING

It would be foolish to pretend that *Chances and Choices* has the 'answer' to integration. That would imply that integration is a problem which needs an answer! Integration itself isn't a problem, but the process of implementing it may be more difficult in some communities than others, for some people more than for others and at some times more than others.

Although each integration situation has individual aspects, it also has many similarities to integration in other communities. *Chances and Choices* has drawn together these common threads of integration. Many of these threads are strands of success that can be shared and act as an example to other communities. Other threads are the knots of difficulties. Because similarities *do* exist, communities are able to help each other by sharing their strands of success—positive experiences, 'handy hints' and practical strategies. Likewise they can share their knots of difficulties; hopefully they can also share their solutions.

Difficulties are often expressed in similar ways—'I don't know where to start' or 'I haven't got enough resources'—but their causes may not be similar because integration is a dynamic process that is different in each community. Each community has a unique blend of people and resources, of experiences and attitudes, of fears and hopes.

'Successful communities recognise difficulties as problems to overcome' (chapter 17). They don't avoid, ignore or escape difficulties; they learn how to overcome them. They use their own experiences and the experiences of other communities to address difficulties so that the principles of integration remain firm.

This chapter lists a number of recurring difficulties and a variety of ways to approach each one.

'I don't know where to start' say the parents of a person with a disability. These parents can be helped to define what they want for their child: Integration where? Why? What do they want the community to offer? They need to understand how integration happens (chapter 3) and how other people may feel about it (chapter 4); then they can start by choosing a community (chapter 5).

'I don't know where to start' says a staff member. Staff members need to understand what integration really is, what it offers and how it happens (chapters 1, 2 and 3). They can find out about their community's experience with integration (chapter 6). They need to keep other people's perspectives (chapter 4) in mind; they can then establish an individual planning committee to set some common goals and develop an individual integration program (chapter 8).

'How do I know whether integration will work at (community X)?'
say the parents of a person with a disability. It is hard to ascertain a community's willingness and capacity (or unwillingness and incapacity) to make integration work, but some signs seem to indicate the likelihood that integration will work (chapter 5). Integration is more likely to work and keep working in any community if effective processes are used (chapter 10).

'We are not ready for integration' say staff; 'The staff are panicking'
say community members. Staff need to understand what integration really is, what it offers and how it happens (chapters 1, 2 and 3). They may need preparation (chapter 7) for a particular person's integration. They need to understand that they can share the responsibility for integration by establishing an individual planning committee to develop goals and a program and to select appropriate resources (chapters 8 and 9).

'This person is not ready for integration'. People need to understand what integration really is, what if offers, how it happens (chapters 1, 2 and 3) and the notion of 'readiness' (chapter 7). By talking about readiness, some people are really asking for more preparation (chapter 7) for themselves, regardless of the perceived readiness of the person with the disability. They can be helped to define more realistic goals and to develop a program to meet those goals (chapter 8).

'But what is he getting out of it—he's only a passive observer'.
Some people participate in community activities in ways that are unlike the participation of other people—they may do more touching, more observing or more practising. Some people are limited in the ways they can participate or interact, perhaps because of sensory or physical disabilities. They may learn in these different ways in any environment in which they participate; another environment won't necessarily help them learn in more ordinary ways. Integration provides them with opportunities to touch, observe and practise ordinary things and to have everyday experiences.

'They don't interact much'. People making this statement recognise that community attendance and program participation are only the beginnings of integration. They recognise the need for interaction and interdependence between community members, and hopefully for friendship. Particular program content and formats (chapter 11) can assist this.

'I don't have enough resources' say staff. The resource checklist can be used to assess resource needs and to ensure their appropriate use

Community member interaction

(chapter 9). An individual planning committee shares the responsibility for the program and its resources.

'It's too complicated for me'.   People may think 'How complicated— overall goals, specific objectives, programs, resources. All I wanted to do was get John to go down to the fast food bar on his own.' People may not want the formality of goals and objectives, and believe that other community members don't want to be part of program planning, either. However an individual planning committee of only one person can still use the factors in chapters 7 (preparation), 8 (programs) and 9 (resources) to help achieve integration for John in the fast food shop.

- *Preparation*: Can John locate the items he wants? Can he manage the shop door, reach the shelf?
- *Specific objectives*: Should John just give the money to the shop-keeper or should he check his change too? Will he go all the way to the shop from home or only from the shop entrance?
- *Program content*: Consider money recognition, using a wallet, recog-nising the goods, asking for goods appropriately and knowing the route to the shop.
- *Resources*: Would a shopping trolley or a basket be best?

'But an individual integration program makes a big fuss. I thought that integration was supposed to be low-key'. Integration is best if it is low-key, in the background, not the foreground. An individual integration program need not make a big fuss about integration. It is not a whole new program that differs from the program of other community members. It is a unique combination of all the community programs that have been individualised for the needs of a particular person. It isn't implemented in a way that stresses 'difference' or 'high profile'; it is implemented in a way that allows community attendance and program participation to be supported by attitudes that promote interaction and interdependence.

'I haven't got the time to do all that's required' says a staff member. The individual planning committee (chapter 8) must develop a realistic individual integration program. A program and resource review (chapters 8 and 9) can examine the effectiveness of resources (like staff) and adjust the program accordingly. Reviews are most effective if good communication, meeting and decision-making processes (chapter 10) are used to enhance shared communication, shared goals and shared responsibility; sharing allows people to express their concerns and to be heard.

'She needs so much time. What do I do with the other group members?' says a staff member. Each community member is entitled to an equal share of staff time and resources. When a community member has additional human resource needs, these need not all be supplied by staff (chapter 9). Particular program formats (chapters 9 and 11) may not only provide additional resources but may develop interaction and interdependence between community members.

'It's too risky'. People need to understand what integration really is, what it offers and how it happens (chapters 1, 2 and 3); integration is a process based on individual needs, a process that responds to individual abilities and difficulties. People may need information about the dignity of risk (chapter 1), and the processes of risk—of self-determination versus protection (chapter 10).

'They keep saying it's a trial period' say the parents of a person with a disability. Staff and parents need to have a mutual understanding of the purpose of any 'trial period' and of how it will be managed (chapter 7). After the trial period, renegotiation can lead to common realistic goals (chapter 8) and appropriate resources to support those goals.

'People aren't doing their job properly'. The individual planning committee (chapter 8) works most effectively by using good communication processes (chapter 10) so that the responsibility for integration is shared. Human resources used for integration should each have a clearly defined role that is regularly reviewed (chapter 9). Staff and committee members may need to be assertive (chapter 15) in negotiating with re-source services to maintain appropriate human resources.

'He's not happy'. Happiness may not be a guide to the success of integration and certainly unhappiness is not a reason to reject integration. Unhappiness has an underlying cause that can be addressed by the use of effective processes (chapter 10), perhaps by encouraging interaction be-tween community members (chapter 11) or by reviewing the individual integration program (chapter 8).

'It won't last long. As she gets older, her friends will drop away'. If the interdependence aspect of integration can be achieved, then friendships can be formed which will survive the changes of time and circumstances. People's interests may change but their friendships can be renegotiated to accommodate this. When only program attendance or program participation has been achieved, then relationships are more superficial and fleeting, and will probably not last beyond the community or if circumstances change.

'How will my other children manage if Jane joins them at their community?' Careful consideration of communities can often provide information about the community or about the person with the disability that will assist her integration to work (chapter 5). Each situation is unique, and the attendance of other family members at a particular com-munity may influence people either towards or away from that community.

'I'm not getting anywhere' says a staff member. Identification of objectives is needed in order to identify progress that is made towards them (chapter 8). Realistic goals and objectives are part of an appropriate individual integration program. Social skills may be important objectives, but progress towards them may be less obvious than towards concrete objectives. Facilitating social skill development is an important aspect of integration that is often unrecognised and undervalued.

'I'm not sure if his difficulties are related to his adolescence or his disability'. People making this statement recognise the individuality of situations, and are keeping disability in perspective. People in resource networks or resource services (chapter 9) may be able to help isolate the underlying difficulties.

'It's not working'. Integration processes and programs can be reviewed to make sure that they do work and continue to work (chapter 17). Sometimes difficulties with integration relate to difficulties that people are having in their lives that have nothing to do with disability or integration: the challenges of adolescence, health problems, career uncertainties, fami-ly crises. These 'ordinary' difficulties may be complicated when a person has a disability, but their very 'ordinariness' may also indicate that integra-tion is providing ordinary experiences that are common to a lot of people.

'I want to know whether integration is working'. The 'results' of integration are not an argument for accepting it or rejecting it; the 'rightness' of integration is not in question. Integration is merely a way of a community providing its members with the equal chances and choices that they all deserve, that they are all entitled to. Information about the process of providing those chances and choices to all members, and about the effectiveness of a particular program, is useful information (chapter 17). It can be used to review a community's integration policy (chapter 6) or an individual integration program (chapter 8).

'Other people can do this better than I can' says a staff member. Some staff have had more experience with integration then others but that doesn't mean they are 'better'. All staff should have the opportunity to learn about integration. They are all part of a large community where people with a disability live, play and work; some may be staff members directly involved with a person who has a disability. Learning about integration requires understanding what integration really is, what it offers and how it happens (chapters 1, 2 and 3).

'A special community would be better'. People need to understand what integration offers people who have a disability and other community members (chapter 2)—integration is a process based on individual needs, that responds to individual abilities and difficulties. By suggesting a special community, some people are really saying 'I don't know where to start' or 'I don't want to do this'. They may need help to identify skills that they would like to develop (chapter 9).

'But that community doesn't have experience with the 'special' resources needed'. (Perhaps braille or behaviour modification). Areas for staff development should be identified, along with other appropriate resources (chapter 9). A transition program (chapter 8), a well organised orientation period (chapter 7) or a period of shared attendance (chapter 8) can be useful.

Difficulties need to be recognised, not ignored; they need to be dealt with, not avoided. Of course integration will have its difficulties and problems, and not all problems have solutions. However successful integration establishes effective processes that keep integration going.

CONCLUSION

Integration *can* work. Integration can provide equal chances and choices to all community members. It can provide a *choice* of communities to attend and programs in which to participate; it can provide the *chance* to interact and to develop interdependent friendships. It may not be easy, but integration can work.

Integration may mean something different to you or to me; integration may look different in this community or in that one; integration may feel different for this person or for that. But it is not a vague dream of tomorrow.

Integration is a reality that is here today, a reality that you and I can be part of. Integration is a process that changes through time and circumstances, and more importantly, can be developed through the attitudes and efforts of people like you and me. Integration works when talk turns into action, when you and I get integration started, up and going, and when everyone works to keep it going.

Community member interdependence

REFERENCES

1 COLLINS, M. (chairman). *Integration in Victorian education*. Report of the review of educational services for the disabled. Victoria: Australian Government Publishing Service, 1984.

2 NIRJE, B. The basis and logic of the normalization principle. *Australian and New Zealand Journal of Developmental Disabilities* 1985: 11:2.

3 FULLWOOD, D. Early intervention—the parent's perspective. In: Johnston, C (ed). *Proceedings of the fourth conference of the New South Wales Early Intervention Association*. Sydney: Early Intervention—a transdisciplinary approach, 1986:26–51

4 CAVANAGH, J, ASHMAN, A. Stress in families with handicapped children. *Australian and New Zealand Journal of Developmental Disabilities* 1985: 11:3.

5 FULLWOOD, D, CRONIN, P. *Facing the crowd: managing other people's insensitivities to your disabled child*. Burwood, Victoria: Royal Victorian Institute for the Blind, 1986. (Burwood educational series no 7).

6 Report reveals opposition to disabled living in community. *The Age*, 1988 January 12.

7 FIELD, M. (ed) Sometimes what others say hurts. In: Field, M. *Making the most of it*. Adelaide: Disabled People's International 1984: 54–55.

8 HERINK, N, LEE, P. Patterns of social interactions of mainstreamed preschool children: hopeful news from the field. *The Exceptional Child* 1985: 32:3

9 SEABORN, T. Freeing up the timetable. In: Huish, R. (ed). *Integration... A place for everyone*. Victoria 1984 Participation and Equity Program: 33–34.

10 STONE, K. (ed) *Integration action manual*. Victoria: Victorian Advocacy Collective, 1985.

11 STEER, M. Normalisation. What does it mean? *Mental Retardation Newsletter* 1983; 2:5.

12 HUISH, R. Peer tutoring. In: Huish, R. (ed). *Integration... A place for everyone*. Victoria 1984 Participation and Equity Program: 20.

13 HUISH, R. Cooperative Learning. In: Huish, R. (ed). *Integration... A place for everyone*. Victoria 1984 Participation and Equity Program: 18–20.

14 READ, M. Integration! But what about assessment? In: Huish, R. (ed). *Integration... A place for everyone*. Victoria 1984 Participation and Equity Program: 33–34.

GLOSSARY

A

Accommodation unit—community residential unit.

Active learning—learning by doing and experiencing.

Advocacy—the provision of an assistant to represent the interests and rights of a person with a disability.

Advocate—an assistant to protect and represent the rights and interests of a person with a disability.

Agenda—a list of the issues to be discussed at a meeting.

Ascertainment—the term used by some agencies to refer to assessment of a person with a disability used to decide their eligibility for services.

Attendant care—a program of providing care via a personal care attendant employed directly by the person with the disability to assist with non-medical tasks.

B

Behaviour modification—a structured program designed to alter behaviour by altering its consequences.

Buddy system—a volunteer matched to a person with a disability to share activities and promote independence.

C

Categorisation—grouping of people or objects based on similarities.

Citizen advocacy—a community-based program which establishes one-to-one relationships between advocates and adults who have a disability.

Co-acitvity—a teaching format assisting a person's limbs through the desired movement.

Collaborative decision-making—a process where decision-makers share information pertinent to the decision, make a consensus decision and share responsibility for it.

Community—a group of people who come together for a common purpose and who are needed to maintain that purpose.

Community integration committee—a committee of various people within a community who develop the community's plan for integration/integration policy.

Community integration plan—a community's overview of integration applied to their community, listing existing resources.

Community-referenced assessment—assessment of a person's actual abilities and needs in a particular community.

Community-referenced instruction—a program format that uses community experiences and cues to teach and reinforce objectives.

Community-referenced objectives—objectives that relate to a particular person's needs in a particular community.

Community residence/residential unit/house—a house in the community with staff who provide varying levels of special assistance to the people with a disability who live there.

Consensus decision—a decision agreed to by all decision-makers.

Consultative decision-making—a process where decision-makers receive advice from consultants who have no say in the decision and no responsibility for it.

Co-operative learning—a program format where a group of people learn through working on one activity for a common goal.

Criteria—established principles for testing.

Cross-age tutoring—a program format where learning and teaching is shared between community members of different ages.

Curriculum—the arrangement of all the experiences being offered by a community.

D

Delayed attendance—a program format where a person joins a community after the usual starting time for new members.

Descriptive assessment—a description of the skills and abilities a person demonstrates at identified learning experiences (activities or tasks actually undertaken).

Devalued—having little value, unworthy, not as good as.

Deviance—the categorisation of a minority group of people based on a 'difference' which is seen as socially important and undesirable.

Dignity of risk—the personal growth possible through being offered risks, making risky choices and taking responsibility for the success or failure of those choices.

Disability—a restriction or lack of ability to perform an activity in a usual way—often caused by an impairment.

Disability awareness programs—sequential active programs of graded experiences about particular disabilities.

E

Equal opportunity—the notion of all people having equal rights.

Equipment library—a library of equipment for loan.

F

Functional learning—a program format of learning skills in ordinary circumstances as the need for those skills arises.

G

Generalisation—the ability to apply a skill learnt in one situation to a variety of other similar situations.

Graded programs/experiences—program content of varying levels of difficulty.

H

Handicap—a disadvantage resulting from an impairment or disability.

I

Impairment—a loss or abnormality of body organ or body function.

Individual integration program—a unique combination of all the community programs which have been individualised for the needs of a particular person.

Individual planning committee—a committee that develops an individual integration program to provide a person with maximum chances and choices at the community.

In-service—staff education on the employment site.

Integration policy—a community's plan for integration.

Integration—a process which offers a person who has a disability the same chances and choices as other people to participate in life's activities and to become a full member of life's communities.

Itinerant teacher—a visiting teacher without a fixed school or class.

L

Lateral thinking—a problem-solving process involving looking at a situation afresh and reducing the problem to its basic elements.

Least restrictive environment/alternative—a system for evaluating choices, by choosing the one that intrudes least on a person's life.

Leisure buddies—a program matching a person with a disability with a volunteer to share friendship and new activities.

M

Majority-rule decisions—a decision supported by the majority of committee members.

Minutes—a written record of a meeting.

Mixed-ability groups—a group of people with varying abilities.

Multisensory learning/instruction—a program format/instructions that use all body senses.

N

Natural consequences—the usual community response to a situation.

Natural learning—learning through ordinary circumstances in a community.

Negative value—undesirable.

Negotiation—a decision-making process aiming for mutual benefit through consensus.

Non-categorisation—not categorising; not presuming that people with one similar characteristic will be similar in all respects.

Non-graded programs—a program format where particpants are not later evaluated on the program content they have learnt.

Non-segregation—not segregating; not isolating some people from normal community activities, chances and choices.

Norm—the performance of an average person.

Normalisation—a process to help people develop valued skills and a valued social image by providing them with normal community conditions and circumstances.

Norm-referenced assessments—standardised assessments where a person's performance is compared to norms.

O

Objective—a statement describing how to reach a particular goal.

Open employment—employment in an ordinary community with ordinary conditions.

Op-shop—a charity shop.

Ordinary community—regular community.

Orientation—the process of becoming familiar with a community.

P

Parent advocacy—advocacy for the parents of a person with a disability.

Part-time attendance—a program format of attendance at a community for less time than other community members usually attend.

Peer modelling—learning from watching and interacting with other people.

Peer support—a program format using an older community member to assist junior members to learn the social aspects of a community.

Peer tutoring—a program format where learning and teaching is shared between community members.

Personal care attendant—a person employed through an attendant care scheme.

Positive value—desirable.

Pre-requisite—a basic requirement.

Program content—the knowlege and skills available through the subjects and experiences offered in a community.

Program format—the grouping and presentation of program content; how program content is taught to community members.

Pub—bar.

R

Regular community—a community of people with a diversity of interests, abilities and lifestyles.

Residential unit—community residential unit.

Resource service—a service available to communities to assist with integration.

Reverse integration—a community primarily for people with a disability attended by some people without a disability.

Role play—an interpersonal technique of practising a 'role' before it is needed.

S

Segregated community—a community of people who have been segregated (usually based on categorisation of them).

Segregation—separation of some people from others (usually based on categorisation).

Self-advocacy—advocacy for yourself; learning to speak for yourself and represent your own rights.

Self-determination—the right to make choices about one's own life.

Self-esteem—the value a person places on his/her self.

Self-paced programs—a program format where people use program content at their own individual rate.

Self-talk—the words people say to themselves, often sub-consciously.

Self-teaching programs—a program format using structured materials that don't need staff to teach them.

Shared attendance—a program format of attendance at two communities, each on a part-time basis.

Sheltered employment—employment with different conditions to a similar job in open employment.

Sheltered workshop—a special employment unit where conditions differ to open employment.

Shouting a round of drinks—buying drinks for a group of people.

Social justice—a belief that all people have equal value.

Social role valorisation—normalisation; a process to help people develop valued skills and a valued social image by providing them with normal community conditions and circumstances.

Social value—the value that community members put on an activity, ability or characteristic.

Social visit—a program format of attendance at a community for a short period, usually with only limited participation expected.

Special services—services developed for people in a minority group.

Special units—a unit for a person with a disability that is within a regular community, and usually with different conditions to the regular community.

Stigma—long-lasting negative social value.

Supported accommodation—accommodation in a regular community but with assistance to fulfil some aspects of domestic living.

Supported employment—open employment but with assistance to meet the conditions expected.

T

Task analysis—a process of goal-directed step-by-step teaching.

Toy library—a library of toys for loan.

Transition program—a program that bridges a change in community or program for a person with a disability.

Trial period—a period of temporary attendance at a community.

V

Visiting teacher—itinerant teacher.

W

Withdrawal program—a program format providing program content away from the regular program location.

Work enclave—a special employment unit providing supported employment to a group of employees in a regular workplace.

Work training unit—a special unit providing training in work skills.

Z

Zero order skill—a skill that is unnoticed when present since it is taken for granted, but its absence is noted.

INDEX